R. ALBERT MOHLER, JR.

ACTS 13-28 FOR YOU

thegoodbook
COMPANY

To
Marvin and Mary Kahler

I did not realize that when I married your precious and beautiful daughter, I would be received so graciously as your son, and join your wonderful family.

Your commitment to Christ and your love for the church have sustained us. Your love for each other and for your children and grandchildren and great-grandchildren inspires us. Your steadfastness undergirds us.

Dad was taken from us far too soon, but our memory of him is precious.

Mom, at age 94, you remain, as always, a marvel.

Thank you. Always.

Acts 13–28 For You

© R. Albert Mohler, Jr., 2019.

Published by:
The Good Book Company

thegoodbook.com I www.thegoodbook.co.uk
thegoodbook.com.au I thegoodbook.co.nz I thegoodbook.co.in

(Hardcover) ISBN: 9781909919952
(Paperback) ISBN: 9781909919945

Printed in India

Design by André Parker

CONTENTS

SERIES PREFACE

Each volume of the *God's Word For You* series takes you to the heart of a book of the Bible, and applies its truths to your heart.

The central aim of each title is to be:

- Bible centered
- Christ glorifying
- Relevantly applied
- Easily readable

You can use *Acts 13–28 For You:*

To read. You can simply read from cover to cover, as a book that explains and explores the themes, encouragements and challenges of this part of Scripture.

To feed. You can work through this book as part of your own personal regular devotions, or use it alongside a sermon or Bible-study series at your church. Each chapter is divided into two (or occasionally three) shorter sections, with questions for reflection at the end of each.

To lead. You can use this as a resource to help you teach God's word to others, both in small-group and whole-church settings. You'll find tricky verses or concepts explained using ordinary language, and helpful themes and illustrations along with suggested applications.

These books are not commentaries. They assume no understanding of the original Bible languages, nor a high level of biblical knowledge. Verse references are marked in **bold** so that you can refer to them easily. Any words that are used rarely or differently in everyday language outside the church are marked in **gray** when they first appear, and are explained in a glossary toward the back. There, you'll also find details of resources you can use alongside this one, in both personal and church life.

Our prayer is that as you read, you'll be struck not by the contents of this book, but by the book it's helping you open up; and that you'll praise not the author of this book, but the One he is pointing you to.

Carl Laferton, Series Editor

Bible translations used:

- ESV: English Standard Version (this is the version being quoted unless otherwise stated)
- NIV: New International Version, 2011 edition

INTRODUCTION TO ACTS 13 - 28

Acts 13 marks a watershed moment in the narrative of the early church. In the first volume of this expository guide, we left off at Acts 12, where Luke began to shift the focus of his story from Peter and the church in Jerusalem to Paul and Barnabas, who would take the gospel to Gentile lands. Indeed, where chapters 1 – 12 chronicled the birth and growth of the Jerusalem church, chapters 13 – 28 recount the advance of the gospel throughout the Roman Empire.

In Acts 1:8, Jesus said to his disciples, "But you will receive power when the Holy Spirit has come upon you, and you will be my witnesses in Jerusalem and in all Judea and Samaria, and to the end of the earth." The latter half of Acts tells the story of the Holy Spirit's work through Paul, Barnabas, and many others who bore witness to the gospel as it began to extend to the ends of the earth. God will have a people as his own from every tribe, tongue, and nation.

In these chapters, we will travel with Paul throughout the Roman Empire as he preaches the gospel, and plants and encourages churches, and then is arrested for his faithfulness to Christ. In Acts 9 Paul (formerly known as Saul) set out to persecute the church of Jesus Christ, but then the Lord appeared to him on the road to Damascus. Saul was converted to faith in Christ and then emerged as the great apostle to the Gentiles. Acts 13 – 28 will reveal the transformative power of God's saving grace as he took a former opponent of the gospel and made him into one of its greatest heralds.

This volume will cover the story of God's overflowing mercy not only to Paul but to all believers in Jesus Christ. God reveals in these chapters that he uses broken, sinful people to accomplish his purposes in salvation history. This is a humbling privilege. This is unspeakable grace—the holy God of the cosmos rescues us out of our sin and rebellion, and refashions us into ambassadors for his kingdom. As he commissioned Paul to take the gospel to the nations, so he also calls

---

* Words in gray are defined in the Glossary (page 197).

all his redeemed children into his service to bear witness to the gospel of Jesus Christ. The church's obedience to our Lord's command in Acts 1:8 is dramatically revealed in this second half of the book.

We also learn that true gospel ministry often meets enormous suffering, trials, and opposition. Indeed, as we will see in the coming chapters, where you find the kingdom of God advancing, you find mounting spiritual opposition. Yet despite the forces that seek to thwart Paul and his missionary journeys, we shall see how God proves himself faithful repeatedly. Nothing will overcome God's will. Nothing can oppose his purposes.

> Where you find the kingdom of God advancing, you find mounting spiritual opposition.

These chapters, therefore, possess an abundance of spiritual nourishment and theological edification for the contemporary church. They provide at least three vital lessons for the church in our day: a church that, much like the church of Paul's day, faces fierce opposition, in our case from the secular forces of modernity.

First, Acts 13 – 28 reveals the need for God's people to be zealous in gospel ministry. In Acts 20, Paul delivers his famous farewell address to the Ephesian elders. In verse 24, Paul says, "But I do not account my life of any value nor as precious to myself, if only I may finish my course and the ministry that I received from the Lord Jesus, to testify to the gospel of the grace of God." Paul laid his life down for the gospel of Jesus Christ. He measured the value of his life by his fidelity to the mission given him by God. Paul's zeal for God's glory shines in every chapter. This is a lesson for every Christian, not just for full-time pastors and missionaries. Zeal for God and his gospel ought to mark every disciple of Jesus Christ. God has saved us out of darkness and made us ambassadors of his kingdom. This mission demands an ardent passion for God and his glory—a passion that overcomes the fiercest opposition and suffering.

Second, Luke details in these chapters the power of the Holy Spirit. While zeal for God must grip every disciple, the Holy Spirit must empower us. Indeed, our hope for fruitfulness hinges upon the work of the Spirit. We can muster all our energy and passion for any task, but if we do not have the Spirit, we will crumble beneath the weight of opposition. All efforts apart from the Holy Spirit will fail. Acts 13 – 28 tells the incredible story of Spirit empowerment—how a group of unlikely men and women utterly changed the world because they possessed the Spirit and the Holy Spirit possessed them. These chapters ought to drive us to our knees in prayer. Where you find a church in triumph, you find a people dependent upon the Holy Spirit's direction and empowerment.

Third, Acts 13 – 28 will reveal that the church must be marked by an unshakeable trust in the sovereign power of God, especially in the face of suffering. In almost every chapter, the reader would expect Paul to meet his end or to surrender to defeat as again and again he faces fierce persecution. He is frequently beaten, stoned and left for dead, shipwrecked, and often held by prisoners' chains. Yet despite the enormous opposition Paul faces, God's sovereign rule uses Paul's suffering in glorious ways. Acts reminds us that God is with us, even in our suffering for the gospel.

These chapters, therefore, remind Christians that discipleship means difficulty—a life of ease, comfort, and prosperity does not await people zealous for God and his kingdom. Quite the contrary—Acts shows us the immense suffering that awaits the faithful servants of Christ. Yet, despite that suffering, it reveals the glorious grace, mercy, and power of God. While Paul faced what seemed like certain death at several points during his ministry, he pressed on with an unspeakable joy; he knew that he lived as a citizen of heaven and that his inheritance lay safe in the courts of heaven under the protection of God himself. No thief could steal Paul's treasure; no moth could destroy it. So Paul lived zealously, trusting in the promises of God. He relied upon the Spirit. He clung to God.

This is the story of Acts 13 – 28. As we progress through these pages of holy Scripture, may God use his word to make us more zealous for his kingdom, to show us our need for his Holy Spirit, and to help us trust in him as we, in our turn, face trials and suffering in the cause of the gospel. For while the Book of Acts tells the story of the earliest years of the church of Jesus Christ, it is not only the story of the apostles and the earliest churches. It is the story of the church—the church that Jesus Christ established and to which he promised that the gates of hell shall not prevail against it. Thus, this is the story that now continues in your church. May God encourage Christ's church through this continuing study of the book of Acts.

1. TOWARD THE ENDS OF THE EARTH

Acts 13 begins a phase of the book which centers upon the missionary journeys of the **apostle** Paul. These chapters do not merely chronicle the geographic movements of a faithful apostle. They demonstrate the power of the gospel as it advances throughout the Mediterranean world and beyond. This mass movement of the gospel, however, began when the people of God sought his name through fasting and prayer (**13:2***).

Luke begins the narrative by summarizing the ministry and the status of the church in Antioch (**v 1**). Luke includes these details to indicate the growing influence of Antioch as a hub of Christian activity. In so doing, Luke sets Antioch up as an equal to Jerusalem in terms of influence in the Christian world.

After Luke records some of the leaders there in Antioch, he writes, "While they were ministering to the Lord and fasting, the Holy Spirit said, 'Set apart for me Barnabas and Saul for the work to which I have called them'" (**v 2**). As the church fasted and sought the face of the Lord through prayer, God interrupted their prayers and answered. The Holy Spirit spoke his will: the **consecration** of Barnabas and Paul for a glorious mission of gospel proclamation.

This meeting in Antioch was true fellowship. Churches today often settle for a watered-down vision of fellowship which typically includes

---

* All Acts verse references being looked at in each chapter part are in **bold**.

eating a meal and talking about the newest movies and latest professional sport developments. This is not biblical fellowship. True fellowship radiates the glories of Christ through prayer and love. At this prayer meeting in Antioch, God answered and set apart two men who would turn the world upside down. Never underestimate the power of true fellowship when God's people gather together in prayer.

The story continues as the church **laid their hands** on Barnabas and Saul, and sent them to Seleucia and Cyprus (**v 3-4**). After praying over them, they sent them on their way to the seaport of Antioch in order to begin their mission in Cyprus, the home of Barnabas (4:36). Once they were on Cyprus, Luke records three things of significance.

1. The Strategy

Luke tells us in **13:5** that Barnabas and Saul began to preach the word of God in the synagogues. These people already believed in God and in the Scriptures. Barnabas and Saul, as Jewish men, would have shared a common religious background with those at the synagogue. Saul and Barnabas, therefore, were leveraging the common ground they shared with Jews toward proclaiming the gospel. This strategy of preaching first to the Jews demonstrates the careful and reasoned approach that Saul and Barnabas took as they sought to advance the gospel of Christ throughout the Mediterranean world. Their gospel preaching began in the synagogues.

2. John Mark

Barnabas and Saul enlisted the help of John to serve as an aide and apprentice in their gospel work (**v 5**). This John was John Mark, the author of the Gospel of Mark. Saul and Barnabas would have had no indication that God would use John Mark as an **inspired** author of the New Testament. This short introduction to John Mark shows how God can powerfully use brief encounters and relationships in order to extend his kingdom. Every glorious end has humble beginnings.

3. Saul to Paul

Our missionaries make their way to Paphos, which served as the territorial seat of power and the location of the governor's palace (**v 6**). While in this influential city, they find a man named Bar-Jesus, meaning son of Jesus or son of Joshua, a common name during that time (**v 6-7**). What should strike the reader as uncommon, however, is the oxymoron of a Jewish magician. Jews, according to several Old Testament texts, should have nothing to do with sorcery, divining, or magic.

Saul and Barnabas find this magician as they come to proclaim the gospel to Sergius Paulus, the proconsul of the region (**v 7**). The magician begins to oppose them by influencing the proconsul away from the message of the gospel (**v 8**). This kind of anti-missionary effort will span the rest of the narrative of Acts. This does not, however, deter Paul and Barnabas from proclaiming the good news. No amount of persecution, hostility, or rejection will hinder their zeal for gospel proclamation.

In **verse 9** Luke writes, "But Saul, who was also called Paul…" Why did Luke start referring to Saul as Paul? Notice, this is not a new name given to Paul. The text says he was already "called Paul." Thus, Paul's parents probably gave him several names at his birth. Saul would have been his Jewish name, while Paul was his Roman name. Luke shows the reader that Saul, now Paul, will have a mission which increasingly departs from Jewish lands and people, and ventures into the Gentile world. Paul will live as the grand missionary and apostle to the Gentiles.

The text continues to show us how Paul, filled with the Spirit, deals with this Jewish sorcerer. Paul says, "You son of the devil, you enemy of all righteousness, full of all deceit and villainy, will you not stop making crooked the straight paths of the Lord?" (**v 10**) This verse succinctly delineates the nature of theological confusion and heresy. Theological error abounds with subversive deceit and flows directly from the lies of Satan himself. Heresy opposes righteousness and aims to confuse the commands, teachings, and character of the Lord our God.

Judgment comes to Elymas in the form of blindness (**v 11**). Through this display of God's power and through the preached word, the proconsul repents and believes in Jesus Christ as his Savior (**v 12**). Paul and Barnabas leave Cyprus, without John Mark (**v 13**), making their way to Pisidian Antioch (**v 14**). Perhaps John had reservations about an **evangelistic** push toward Gentile lands. This would explain the bitterness and conflict which erupts later in Acts between Paul and Barnabas when John tries to rejoin the team (15:39).

The Mission Moves to Galatia

Once Paul and Barnabas make it to Pisidian Antioch, a city in the region of Galatia, they enter the synagogue and listen to the reading of the Scriptures (**13:15**). Then, the official asks if Paul has any word or exhortation for the present congregation. As Paul begins his sermon, he stands up and motions with his hand (**v 16**). Peter, in just the previous chapter, also motioned with his hand before he spoke. Luke includes these details in order to parallel Peter and Paul as the two foundational apostolic preachers of the first-century church.

Paul begins his sermon by stating, "Men of Israel and you who fear God..." (**v 16**). Paul reveals the diversity of his crowd. Not only are ethnic Jews present but Gentile converts also fill the synagogue. Paul's content resembles that of **Stephen's** sermon in Acts chapter 7.

13:17-22: In these verses, Paul takes his audience back to the book of Genesis. When asked if he has a word of exhortation, Paul takes them back to the very beginning because the foundation of the gospel itself is in the dawning of creation.

Verses 23-25: Up to this point, Paul's message would have resonated with his audience. Paul has established his message on the common ground he shares with the Jews. Common ground only serves as a launching pad, not a place of rest. He knows he has to confront his audience with the truth, and indeed, the offense, of the full gospel message. He does this here, where he indicates that the promises of God have been fulfilled in Christ Jesus. The one that the nation of Israel longed for has come and secured salvation, not only for the Jews but for the entire world. Christians must learn from Paul's style of presentation. On the one hand, he exuded empathy as he grounded his message in something that his audience would have understood. On the other hand, Paul advanced his message to the uniqueness of Christ, which would have required courage and conviction. Christians need both empathy and courage in order to present the gospel effectively, persuasively, and passionately.

> We need both empathy and courage if we are to present the gospel effectively.

Verses 26-27: In **verse 27**, Paul condemns the actions of the Jerusalem leaders who rejected the **Messiah**. However, Paul roots the identity of Jesus in the very Scriptures which the community hears read every **Sabbath**. He also tells his audience that Jesus' rejection in Jerusalem fulfilled the prophetic pronouncements contained in the holy word.

Verses 28-34: In these verses, Paul recounts the death, burial, and resurrection of Jesus Christ. Paul recognizes that these events have brought to fruition the entire redemptive plan of God in the Scriptures and have secured the good news of eternal salvation. Paul reveals how all of God's word points to the **Christ** who was to come and the ministry of Jesus.

Verses 35-37: Paul contrasts the life of **David** with the life of Jesus. In **verse 35**, Paul quotes Psalm 16:10, which would seem to be a promise for King David. Paul reveals in Acts **13:36-37**, however, that the promise of Psalm 16:10 yearned for its fulfillment in a greater David to come. That psalm could not have been about David. David's bones are dust. It had to be about the one David saw. It had to be about the One from David's line: the true, lasting and eternal fulfillment of all God's promises.

Acts 13:38-39: We come to understand the significance of Paul's words in these verses when we remember his audience: Jews, who thought salvation came through works of the law. The Bible teaches the inability of the law to save. Galatians 2:16 says, "Yet we know that a person is not justified by works of the law but through faith in Jesus Christ ... by works of the law no one will be justified." Romans 3:20 says, "For by works of the law no human being will be justified in his sight, since through the law comes knowledge of sin." The law could not save because of the power of sin. The law does not provide salvation but points to the need for salvation. Paul, therefore, preached the chain-breaking power of Christ's ministry, which secures freedom for all who believe in his name. Salvation comes not by works but by faith in the One who fulfilled the law's demands perfectly.

Acts 13:40-41: Paul's concluding words reveal the incredible significance of responses to the preached word. Paul shows us that there is no such thing as a neutral response to the gospel. The gospel demands repentance and faith in Jesus Christ; anything less amounts to a rejection of God's grace and provision through the cross of his Son.

A Watershed Move in the Gospel Mission

The people of Pisidian Antioch initially responded to the gospel with acceptance. Indeed, "nearly the whole city assembled" to hear Paul and begged him to continue preaching the words of life (**v 42-44**). This response created a problem for the Jewish leaders, who simmered in jealous rage as Paul's ministry flourished (**v 45**). These leaders began to contradict Paul's message. This opposing argument, however, amounted to a **blasphemous** declaration and a rejection of God himself (**v 45**).

Verse 46 contains a stinging indictment by Paul and Barnabas against the Jewish leaders. In this verse, Luke records a massive **missiological** shift—a watershed moment in the Acts narrative. The gospel will advance to the Gentile world. Paul now becomes the apostle to the Gentiles. Indeed, Paul establishes the validity of his mission through the prophetic witness of the "servant songs" of Isaiah 42 and 49 (Acts **13:47**).

While the Jews responded to the word with blasphemy, the Gentiles responded with great joy (**v 48**). In this narrative account, it is the Gentiles, not the Jews, who receive the word with gladness and bring glory to God as they respond to his word with repentance and faith.

Shaking Off the Dust

Verses 49-52 mark the close of the narrative. God spread his word throughout the whole region (**v 49**). As happens so often in the history of the church, great spiritual advancement meets with an equally great spiritual hostility (**v 50**). In this case, the crowds drive out Paul and Barnabas from the entire district. Paul and Barnabas, however, "shook off the dust from their feet in protest against them and went to Iconium" (**v 51**). To shake off the dust from your feet was an act of protest and a physical demonstration of disgust.

Paul's actions in Acts 13 indicate that sometimes in our gospel ministry, we might have to shake off the dust from our feet and move on to other people. Later in Acts, Paul will endure and continue to preach in certain regions even though he will meet a more potent hostility than that which we see here in chapter 13. When, then, should you "shake off the dust from your feet"? That is a question between you and the Spirit of God. This passage does make clear, however, the horrifying consequences which befall those who reject the gospel of Jesus Christ.

How do Paul and Barnabas and the new disciples respond to this persecution and hostility? **Verse 52** says they were filled with joy and the Holy Spirit. They counted it an honor to endure persecution in the name of the gospel. Even in rejection, the gospel was proclaimed.

Modern Western Christians might find it difficult to count it a joy when faithful living provokes persecution. Those who live in faithful obedience to God might think they deserve a better life—a life which rewards their efforts and obedience. When suffering comes, a Christian who genuinely desires to glorify God may still experience deep discouragement and bitterness toward God. The Bible, however, reveals how God uses the suffering of his people to accomplish glorious purposes. Indeed, the history of the church has chronicled a myriad of stories in which, when God's people suffered greatly, God grew his church and his people bore tremendous fruit. Believers can count their suffering as joy because of the God they serve. God does not abandon his children and leave them in the hands of the enemy. God never loses his **sovereign** grip over the lives of his people. While God may bring his people to a season of suffering, he purposes suffering for the expansion of his church. As Paul says in Colossians 1:24, "Now I rejoice in my sufferings for your sake, and in my flesh I am filling up what is lacking in Christ's afflictions for the sake of his body, that is the church." Paul knew that his suffering was joined together with the sufferings of Christ to advance the gospel. That is why he could live joyfully in the midst of suffering for Christ. So can—and so should—we.

Questions for reflection

1. How would you define "fellowship"? What part can you play in your church enjoying the kind of fellowship we find in Acts 13?

2. Acts 13 reveals the significance of our response to the gospel. How might this affect your evangelism and your presentation of the gospel?

3. When might it be time to "shake off the dust from your feet" and proclaim Christ to another person or people? How might you discern the right course of action as you encounter hostility?

PART TWO

In Iconium, our missionaries head straight for the synagogue and begin preaching to the Jews. Paul's words to the Jewish leaders in Acts 13 do not, therefore, preclude the Jewish people as a whole from the **salvific** power of the gospel. Also, as Paul moves into Iconium, he adopts the very same strategy he used on Cyprus and in Antioch by leveraging his Jewish heritage in order to provide a natural place for his gospel proclamation to begin.

Similar Patterns as the Gospel Advances

The pattern of Paul's strategy encounters a similar pattern of belief coupled with opposition (Acts **14:1-2**). Jewish leaders meet the proclamation of the gospel with hostility and respond by inflaming the Gentile rulers of the city against Paul and Barnabas. The Jews who opposed Paul set about inciting the judgment of the Gentile rulers by convincing them that Paul and Barnabas had rebellious motives and sought to lead an uprising.

Despite the machinations of the Jewish leaders, Paul and Barnabas remained in the city for a long time, "speaking boldly for the Lord, who bore witness to the word of his grace, granting signs and wonders to be done by their hands" (**v 3**). This verse enshrines the gospel conviction of Paul and Barnabas, who will not let opposition silence the only message of salvation. Also, this verse testifies to the authority by which the apostles preached. They preached not merely in words but in signs and wonders. The signs God did through Paul and Barnabas served as authenticating marks that demonstrated God's favor upon their message.

Today, Christians can validate the messages of preachers differently: primarily, by assessing the growth and maturity of a congregation. Does the preacher's message point to Christ? Does the preacher focus on the word of God and base his messages on the Scriptures. Is the congregation growing in holiness and in the fruit of the Spirit as a result of the preaching? Such questions can help discern the validity of a preacher and his ministry.

Powerful signs and gospel-saturated preaching, however, left the city divided (**v 4**). The gospel will divide. It can divide nations, cities, towns, villages, and even families. Jesus himself said that he who is not willing to leave father and mother, sisters and brothers, is not worthy of the kingdom of God (Luke 14:26). In other words, the gospel supersedes all earthly commitments and relationships.

Acts **14:5-7** recounts the culmination of opposition as Gentiles and Jews incited their rulers to stone Paul and Barnabas. By God's grace, our missionaries learned of the plot and fled to the cities of Lyconia, Lystra, and Derbe. When the persecution reached a point where their ministry could no longer proceed, they left that area. **Verse 7**, however, reminds us of the singular vision which possessed Paul and Barnabas. They knew what God had called them to do, and nothing would stop them.

Confusing the Message with the Messenger

In **verses 8-15**, Luke homes in on a specific miracle at Lystra which caused uproar in the town. A man had been born with paralysis (**v 8**). The wording Luke uses and the subsequent healing of this paralyzed man (**v 9-10**) take us back to a similar healing in Acts chapter 3, when Peter healed another paralyzed man. Throughout his book, Luke constructs two pillars in the narrative—Peter and Paul. He does this as a literary device, which shows the foundation of the church through Peter and the advancement of the church to the known world through Paul.

The response to the healing of the paralyzed man in Acts chapter 3 differs greatly from the response of the crowds in Acts 14. In Peter's case, his audience was Jewish. In Paul's case, however, he performs this miracle in front of a Gentile audience. The crowd fails to understand what Paul has done and they begin to think that the miracle demonstrates something about Paul rather than something about God. The Gentile audience thinks that Barnabas and Paul must be gods (**v 11-13**). The crowds have confused the message with the messenger.

Luke records the response of Paul and Barnabas in **verse 14**: "When [they] heard of it, they tore their garments." When a person tore their garments, they did so as an act of abject humiliation. At this moment, Paul seizes upon this providential opportunity to clarify the gospel. When the crowds confuse the message with the messenger, they distort the entire gospel.

This scene bears a significant application for the modern church. While few congregations may attempt to crown their preacher as Zeus and offer a sacrifice to their ministers as gods, we can easily erect personality cults which place the preacher upon a pinnacle of perceived authority and infallibility. Christians can and must give respect and honor to their spiritual leaders. That respect, however, slips into hero worship when it overlooks moral failure or lowers standards of godliness. Those who preach and teach the word must realize that they live as mere men like anyone else. Nothing of the divine nature dwells in any minister of the gospel. Paul and Barnabas rebuke the crowds and enjoin them to honor the message, not the messengers.

From Vain Things to a Living God

Verses 15-17 contain a brief sermon of the apostle Paul in which he exposes the desire of human hearts for vanity. As a result of the **fall**, humans possess disordered affections. We long for worthless things, thinking that in them we will find life. The desire for vanity has been exposed long before in the prophetic books of the Old Testament. In Isaiah 44, the prophet ridicules those who make idols out of trees and bow down to an image made by human hands. While we may laugh at the stupidity that would lead someone to worship a tree, make no mistake: the desire for vanity resides deep within our affections. Will money save you? Will a large bank account stop you from falling into the arms of death? Will a successful career provide you with peace, security, and comfort?

Paul's enjoins his audience to "turn from these vain things to a living God" (Acts **14:15**). Notice the contrasting elements Paul presents: on the one hand, vain things; on the other, the living and eternal God. This simple distinction highlights the unsearchable depth of our hardness of heart. Our affections drive us to created things rather than to the Creator. Time and time again in the Old and New Testaments, human ingenuity, human theological "creativity," human superstition, and human philosophy all succumb to an indictment of vanity. Some believe that intellectual sophistication will lead them to knowledge of the truth. They search in vain because what they seek is vain. Truth, and the glories therein, only comes through divine revelation.

Paul's missiological method adapts his gospel presentation to the features and culture of his audience. Paul knows the theological confusion inherent in the people of Lystra and aims to direct the affections of their hearts towards the power of the one true God. He speaks of the "living God, who made the heavens and the earth and the sea and all that is in them." Paul seeks to correct their false conceptions of the universe and the created order by pointing out the authoritative, **omnipotent** creative rule of **Yahweh**. He contrasts the false gods of **pagan** mythology with the infinite God of the universe, who rules over the cosmos and upholds the creation by the word of his power.

Paul strips the pagan gods of their supposed power and authority, stating, "In past generations he allowed all the nations to walk in their own ways. Yet he did not leave himself without witness, for he did good by giving you rains from heaven and fruitful seasons, satisfying your hearts with food and gladness" (**v 16-17**). He shows that the world is not the playground of Zeus, **Aphrodite**, **Hades**, or **Apollo**. The creation, rather, submits to the sovereign rule of the all-powerful God, who spoke all things into existence (**v 17**).

Paul, therefore, dismantles the pagan worldview and offers a theological corrective. He dismisses their pagan worship, sends the priests of Zeus away, deflects their attempt to honor him as a god, and points them to the one true God, who did in fact create the world and has continually provided for them through rain and bountiful harvest seasons. The pagan worldview sought to offer sacrifices in order to appease the gods, and thereby hoped for good harvest seasons. Paul says the true God has already graciously provided those for them, in spite of their idolatrous sacrifices. Moreover, Paul calls them not to offer a sacrifice for a good harvest but to come and know this God personally—to forsake vanity and revel in the resplendent riches of God and his glory.

Despite Paul's mastery in his speech, the crowds still attempt to offer a sacrifice to him and Barnabas as gods (**v 18**). The preacher can preach his heart out, but he cannot raise the dead to life. The darkness which gripped the hearts of the crowd reminds us of the devastation of the fall. Eloquence and flawless wisdom cannot cure spiritual blindness. Paul faithfully preached, but only God can lift the veil.

The Cost of Discipleship

Verse 19 shatters the scene as Paul goes from denying the claim that he is a god to being dragged out of the city and almost stoned to death. Indeed, here Luke says that the Jews won over the crowds and so exposed the fecklessness of the Gentiles' hearts. The Jews from the previous city, still enraged at Paul and Barnabas, seek them out and hope to execute Paul in the most humiliating way. They drag him outside of the city to stone him to death and then to leave his body for the dogs and the birds to feast on.

Luke compresses the history in order to keep the narrative moving. He leaves out certain details that he, and ultimately the Holy Spirit, have deemed unimportant. Luke indicates that there is a group of disciples with Paul—no doubt new believers who have come to Christ through Paul's ministry—and that Paul survives the stoning and re-enters the city.

The next day, his body bruised and broken, Paul, along with Barnabas, departs for Derbe, preaches the gospel and sees many people repent and believe (**v 20-21**). After that Paul and Barnabas backtrack to the places where they have been, "strengthening the souls of the disciples, encouraging them to continue in the faith, and saying that through many tribulations we must enter the kingdom of God" (**v 22**). This concept was not theoretical for Paul. He came to understand, through horrific experiences, the cost of discipleship.

The default position for the church in most of its history has always been the experience of tribulation and persecution. Jesus said in John 15 that the servant is not greater than his master. If Jesus suffered, we must expect the same. Following Christ as a faithful witness comes at a great cost. Most reading this book will not suffer a physical beating for proclaiming the gospel. You may, however, receive a psychological stoning as the culture rejects you and dismisses your religious convictions as an antiquated system of beliefs which clings to a bygone age long ago surpassed by the "glory" of modernity. Paul says, however, that it is through those trials that we will enter the kingdom of heaven. In 2 Corinthians 4, Paul encourages the church by saying that this light, momentary affliction is preparing for us an eternal weight of glory beyond all comparison. Suffering will come. We must endure; for on the other side of tribulation is the sweet embrace of our Savior.

> We endure, for on the other side of tribulation is the sweet embrace of our Savior.

The remainder of the chapter chronicles the return of Paul and Barnabas to Antioch of Syria (Acts **14:21-28**). At each stop on their journey, they encourage the new Christians and appoint **elders** to oversee these new Christian communities and churches (**v 23**). Paul and Barnabas know that for these communities to flourish, they need spiritual leaders present who can carry on the task of leading others to faith and helping other Christians mature in their walk.

Once they return to Antioch of Syria, Paul and Barnabas encourage their sending church and tell them of the glorious testimony of God's saving power (**v 27**). They recount the power of the gospel as it has spread throughout the Mediterranean world. Paul and Barnabas suffered. They could have returned defeated and broken, angry and frustrated that such calamity would befall faithful servants of Christ. Instead, they recognized the glory of suffering. They were counted worthy to suffer for the gospel. God used their suffering as a glorious testimony which strengthened the church of Christ and saw new believers won to the family of God. Indeed, your testimony can produce the same fruit. When you endure suffering and tribulation, you have no idea how God will use your story to encourage others. The testimony of God's suffering saints nourishes the faith of all God's people.

Questions for reflection

1. When you share the gospel with someone, they might recognize that if they believe in Christ, it will divide them from their family or friends. How might you walk them through that difficulty?

2. What theological confusion do you meet in your community or culture? How do you need to adapt the way you explain the gospel, in order to help people understand what you are saying?

3. If someone were to look at your life, would they understand that the way to the kingdom of God includes suffering for the kingdom of God? Why / why not?

2. THE COUNCIL OF JERUSALEM

Acts 15 chronicles the first council in church history. Several councils stand as pillars of **doctrine** and **theological** clarification. The Council of Nicaea in 325 sought to elucidate the nature of **Christology**. In 381, the Council of Constantinople convened to discuss further Christological issues which emanated from the proceedings in Nicaea. The topic of human nature summoned church leaders to another council at Ephesus in 431. The 451 Chalcedonian Council sought to settle issues which flowed from the council at Ephesus. Each of these councils convened over issues of **orthodoxy** and the dissemination of heretical doctrines in **Christendom**. False doctrine assailed the church, and its leaders met to protect that faith once for all delivered to the **saints** (Jude 3).

Much like these **ecumenical councils** which marked the first centuries of the church's history, the Council of Jerusalem in Acts 15 convened over vital matters central to the gospel. Acts 15 teaches us the importance of doctrine and sound teaching. The church in its infancy came under the assault of false teaching. Luke will recount for us in this pivotal chapter the conviction of the apostles and their steadfast theological fidelity. Indeed, Acts 15 distills the danger of doctrinal capitulation: a tainted gospel is no gospel at all. A proclamation of good news laced with heresy will, like a drink mixed with poison, kill the hearer.

Celebration Denied

Acts 14 ended with Paul and Barnabas recounting God's glorious work among the Gentile nations. The good news of the gospel had spread throughout the Mediterranean world. This celebration, however, came to an abrupt halt when false teachers infiltrated the church and sought to squelch the flames of joy kindled by Paul's testimony (**15:1**). Men came down from the region of **Judea** and said, "Unless you are **circumcised** according to the custom of **Moses**, you cannot be saved." These teachers were referred to as Judaizers—Jews who had converted to Christianity but taught obedience to the **Mosaic laws** as necessary for salvation. The concerns of the Judaizers centered on the role of the law in the **new covenant**. Acts 6:14 records the outrage of some Jews who saw that the apostles' teaching and the faith of Christ changed and abolished the customs of Moses. Lest we too quickly jump to judgment, we need to enter into the worldview of the Judaizers in order to grasp the nature of their opposition. The Judaizers saw within the law no mere system of rules. Embedded within the **old covenant** was their identity.

> Judaizers saw within the law no mere system of rules, but their identity.

The Judaizers' message, however, surrendered the glory of the gospel. Paul and Barnabas recognized the danger of the Judaizers' message and "had no small dissension and debate with them" (**15:2**). Paul and Barnabas would not give an inch. They understood that the meaning of the Judaizers' position was deadly to the gospel and would empty it of its power. The Judaizers attempted to add something to the gospel, resulting in the formula *Jesus + works of the law = salvation*. This formula exists today. Catholics believe in Jesus plus the keeping of the **sacraments** as necessary for salvation. Others teach that Jesus plus good works of morality will gain you salvation. Anything, however, which attempts to supplant the complete sufficiency of Christ's **atoning** sacrificing amounts to heresy and a false gospel.

The church at Antioch decided that this matter needed discussing with the church leaders in Jerusalem. They appointed Paul, Barnabas, and others to seek the counsel of the apostles and elders in Jerusalem (**v 2-3**). The Antiochene company recounted to the Jerusalem leaders God's saving grace and power to the Gentiles (**v 4**).

The testimony of the gospel's spread would, again, give cause for celebration. Luke, however, records, "But some believers who belonged to the party of the Pharisees rose up and said, 'It is necessary to circumcise them and to order them to keep the law of Moses'" (**v 5**). Luke provides helpful information about the Judaizers in the crowd.

First, he calls them believers. Sometimes, believers in Christ will have disagreements. Sin still exists and affects our relationships, even with brothers and sisters in Christ. These disagreements do not always necessitate convening the whole church for a council. There might be a heated discussion about the color of the church carpet. That kind of disagreement, however, has more to do with pride in our own hearts than what we see happening in Acts 15. What this chapter does teach us, however, is the reality of conflict that will occur, even between believers. In handling conflict, we need to remember that, if we believe the gospel, we are brothers and sisters, and not enemies.

Second, they belonged to the **Pharisee** party. If we read through the gospels, we see that the Pharisees hated Jesus and devoted themselves to his destruction. Even the apostle Paul had been a Pharisee. The fact that Pharisees repented and believed in Christ should give us cause to rejoice and praise God for his grace. The Judaizers' identity as Pharisees also helps us understand their demand about the law. The Pharisees represented the most conservative faction of the Jews at that time. They also held deep apprehensions about the inclusion among God's people of Gentiles. Conservative Jews would have viewed Gentiles as unclean, and needing to be ceremonially cleansed and circumcised as the law prescribed (Leviticus 12:3). The Jewish Christians, therefore, had a legitimate theological concern, but they came to the wrong conclusion.

The debate continued until a hush fell over the council. Peter, the rock, one of Jesus' closest disciples, stood to address the crowd (Acts **15:7**).

No Distinction

Peter addressed the crowd with a powerful message which established a sound theological answer to the Judaizers and demonstrated the beauty of the gospel in tearing down dividing walls of ethnic identity. Peter grounds his sermon in three key points:

1. *Peter's Vision.* Peter reminds the audience of God's will in selecting Peter to carry the gospel to the first Gentiles (**v 7**). Peter, no doubt, draws the crowd back to the narrative of Acts 10, where God revealed his acceptance of Gentiles and sealed that promise through the conversion of **Cornelius**. Peter knew God's will because God had revealed to him the global advance of the gospel as it extended salvation to the Gentile world.

2. *The Heart Needs Cleansing.* Peter points to the centrality of the heart in the Christian life (**v 8**). He reminds the Judaizers of the inferiority of ceremonial purity compared to a heart cleansed by the blood of Jesus Christ. The new covenant fulfilled the prophetic longing of Ezekiel 36 that God would write his law on the hearts of his people. He would give his children new hearts— alive through the gospel and free from the power of sin. Peter, no doubt, remembered the words of his Master, who also told the Pharisees that the heart defiles a person (Matthew 15:18). What flows from the heart reveals the true character and nature of a person. Jesus taught his disciples the necessity of a new, clean heart. Peter focuses on the heart because the Judaizers believed the law still provided a cleansing power that the gospel did not. The Judaizers, however, operated in the worldview of the Pharisees. A Pharisee would have had great difficulty in ceasing observance of the law, in which Israel's tradition and identity had been

deeply rooted. The law, however, cannot make a person clean. Only the blood of Christ atones for sin.

3. *No Distinction between Jew and Gentile.* Finally, Peter makes clear in Acts **15:9-11** that the gospel has torn down the dividing walls between ethnic groups. The new covenant began a new era in **redemptive history** in which all peoples from all nations and all tribes enjoy the salvific promises fulfilled in Christ. God has abolished the distinction between Jew and Gentile precisely because he cleanses the heart through the perfect sacrifice of the Lamb—the Son of God. Peter, furthermore, sees evidence in the Gentile believers of the Holy Spirit, who is the authenticating seal of God's presence (**v 8**). Furthermore, Peter exposes the hypocrisy of the Jews who would dare to place the burden of the law on Gentiles when the Jews themselves had failed to keep the requirements of the law (**v 10**). Indeed, Peter concludes with the powerful words "We will be saved through the grace of the Lord Jesus, just as they will" (**v 11**). Jew and Gentile alike rest not upon works of the law but on faith in Christ and the grace he extends in eternal salvation.

Peter's threefold focus on his vision, the heart, and the removal of ethnic barriers reveals the immeasurable significance of the Jerusalem deliberations. Paul, Barnabas, and now Peter, understood the danger for the gospel in the Judaizers' teaching. The message of the saving and authentic power of the gospel was at stake.

An Old Promise Fulfilled in Christ

After Peter finishes, Paul and Barnabas recapitulate the spread of the gospel throughout the Gentile world (**v 12**). Upon hearing their testimony, James stands and addresses the assembly (**v 13**). This James was the brother of the Lord Jesus and the author of the biblical book which bears his name. James rose to prominence in the Jerusalem church and served as its primary leader. Having considered the words of Peter (called Simeon here, **v 14**) and Paul, James issues an edict and decides the doctrinal matter. He does so, however, in a surprising way. He grounds the salvation of the Gentiles not in Paul's testimony or Peter's vision but in the Old Testament (**v 15-17**). James, therefore, comes to understand the Gentiles' inclusion in God's people as the fulfillment of a prophecy long ago declared in the Hebrew Scriptures. He quotes from Amos 9:11-12 (for a similar theme, see Jeremiah 12:15). In so doing, James recalls the very voice of God, who spoke through the prophets his plan of redemption, which would rebuild the house of David with a new remnant—a multitude of people from all the nations. When Jesus established the new kingdom, he fulfilled that prophetic promise and founded the restored house of David which would include Jews and Gentiles.

James declares before the assembly a theology and doctrine built upon the Scriptures, revealed by God, and founded in Christ. The Gentiles do not need to keep the circumcision laws prescribed in the Old Testament because Gentile inclusion in the family of God rests on their faith in Christ. James does, however, set out moral instructions for Gentiles to observe (Acts **15:19-21**). The particular instructions he sets out relate to matters of singular offence in the eyes of Jewish believers. In other words, James enjoins Gentiles to love their Jewish brothers and sisters by not intentionally provoking Jews to frustration. James calls upon Gentile Christians not to offend Jews through their actions, by abstaining from "things polluted by idols ... sexual immorality, and from what has been strangled, and from blood" (**v 20**).

This list included items for which Jews reserved the deepest disgust and revulsion. The second item, "sexual immorality," might seem odd given the widespread biblical admonitions to be sexually pure. Why, therefore, would James need to include a command regarding sexual purity if sexual purity was to mark the Christian life regardless of ethnic identity? James, however, lists sexual immorality along with things (probably food) polluted by idols, things that have been strangled, and blood. The context, therefore, indicates that James has in mind **Levitical** commands and laws that Jews viewed as particularly important and necessary. Thus, by "sexual immorality," James probably has in mind the purity and marriage commands listed in Leviticus 18. As John B. Polhill suggests, his reason for including this admonition here may well be because...

> "Gentile sexual mores were lax compared to Jewish standards, and it was one of the areas where Jews saw themselves most radically differentiated from Gentiles. The boundary between ritual and ethical law is not always distinct, and sexual morality is one of those areas where it is most blurred. [Therefore] For the Jew sexual misbehavior was both immoral and impure."
>
> (*Acts* in The New American Commentary Series
> (Holman Reference, 1992), page 330)

So it was important that James underlined this area as one where Gentile obedience to God's law as revealed through his word was of particular importance with regard to safeguarding the unity of God's people, comprising Jewish and Gentile believers.

James' instruction reminds us of Paul in 1 Corinthians 8:13, where he says, "Therefore, if food makes my brother stumble, I will never eat meat, lest I make my brother stumble." Paul humbly submitted himself to the needs of those around him. If his actions could cause any offense, he abstained from those behaviors, even if they were not sinful. Paul's attitude and James' command in Acts 15 call all believers to subordinate personal preferences to the needs of others.

While the council held the line on gospel fidelity and theological conviction, it also revealed the power of the gospel in dismantling ethnic barriers. The church today would do well to study the Jerusalem Council and remember the power of the gospel in unifying a multinational and multiethnic church. Many churches today divide over ethnic and cultural issues. Different ethnicities in the

> We would do well to remember the power of the gospel in uniting a multiethnic church.

same communities can harbor suspicion, and in some cases, bitterness towards other ethnicities. Acts 15, however, should remind and convince churches today of God's intention in the message of the gospel. If the gospel can unite Jews with Gentiles, then it can bridge any divide between any race and ethnicity. May God have mercy on any who would erect a barrier between ethnic groups when God has purposed his gospel to establish a kingdom made up of all tribes, tongues, and nations.

Finally, the council should prompt Christians to assess their own understanding of the gospel. Christians can tend towards a pharisaical view of the gospel in which a focus on their obedience to God has eclipsed their view of and their need for the cross. On the other hand, Christians can presume upon the grace of God, leading to a flippant life which disregards the transformative powers of the gospel. In both cases, Christians need to repent. The former need to know their salvation does not rest in obedience but in Christ. Obedience and faithfulness flow naturally from a person saved by grace. The latter also need the cross, but in order to see the cost of their sin. Jesus paid a terrible price that his people ignore or belittle whenever they view salvation as cheap and holiness as optional, and so choose to live like pagans.

Questions for reflection

1. How do you respond to false teaching? How *should* you respond?

2. What theological differences are enough to break fellowship with people, and which are not? Do you tend toward serious disagreement too quickly or too slowly, do you think?

3. Can you think of a time when you have surrendered your "rights" in order to further the cause of the gospel? How might you be able to do this at present?

PART TWO

Lessons in a Letter

After James concluded, the Jerusalem council concurred and chose men from among themselves as ambassadors for the council. These men would carry a letter throughout the region instructing the disciples and proclaiming the authoritative conclusion of the Jerusalem deliberations. Paul and Barnabas would be accompanied by Judas and Silas, leaders among the council, to deliver the letter (Acts **15:22**).

Verses 23-29 contain the contents of the letter. It recounts much of what has been stated in the prior verses. The fact that Luke records the entirety of the letter demonstrates its theological significance for the early church. Writing books or letters in the ancient world bore a tremendous cost. Each and every word added to the total cost of producing letters. Luke could have merely summarized. Instead, and at a cost, he records the whole letter. Like a good historian, he records in detail the primary sources crucial to his narrative. He wanted the contents of the letter reproduced and preserved in full detail, ensuring the survival of the letter's message and the continuation of its significance.

The letter relates the trouble which the Judaizers caused. It also makes clear that the Judaizers did not come to the Gentile Christians on the authority of the apostles or the leaders of the Jerusalem church (**v 24**). The letter also exudes compassion on the part of the apostles for the Gentile believers. The Jerusalem leaders write, "Some persons have gone out from us and troubled you with words, unsettling your minds." The apostles take note of the difficulty in which the Gentile believers have found themselves as they try and live as faithful disciples. Instead of merely issuing a directive, the apostles exemplify a pastoral concern for the hearts and minds of the Gentile Christians.

The letter also dignifies Paul and Barnabas as beloved brothers in the faith, thereby giving credence to their position in the church (**v 25-26**).

The apostles refer to Paul and Barnabas as "our beloved," indicating the deep affection in which the Jerusalem church held these two men. Indeed, the letter praises the faithfulness of Paul and Barnabas, who, as men zealous for Christ, were willing to die for the sake of the gospel. Christians need heroes of the faith to emulate. The faith of brothers and sisters who have gone before us should inspire all Christians to more faithful service and obedience. Indeed, the author of Hebrews writes, "Remember your leaders, those who spoke to you the word of God. Consider the outcome of their way of life, and imitate their faith" (Hebrews 13:7). Hebrews 13 and the letter from Jerusalem recorded in Acts 15 ground our need for valiant men and women of Christ.

The Holy Spirit Protects the Church

The letter goes on to call the Gentiles to adopt behavior that will show love to their Jewish brothers and sisters (Acts **15:29**). Indeed, rather than demanding conformity, the letter points to the flourishing which will result from following its recommendations. It also gives impetus to its claims by referring to the authority of the Holy Spirit (**v 28**).

The mention of the Holy Spirit provides great comfort for the church. Acts 15 chronicles how God himself protected the bride of Christ—the church—from erroneous teachings which would harm the spread of the gospel. At times, Christians embody an ungodly fear of the world and can slip into believing that the world will overcome the church. Heresy is found everywhere. False teachers spin their webs of lies and deceit. The world increasingly exudes a particular and vitriolic hostility toward Christ-centered, Bible-believing churches. In the context of Acts 15, false teaching troubled many believers. The letter from the Jerusalem Council, however, dispels any notion of fear and proclaims the role of the Holy Spirit in protecting the church and its doctrine. Take heart and know that God will not forsake his church. His eternally powerful Spirit will forever protect the body of Christ from false teaching, impure doctrine, and the schemes of Satan.

The Holy Spirit's role in the Acts 15 narrative should lead believers towards a sole dependence on God. The Scriptures attest to our need for God. Indeed, in John 15 v 5, Jesus told his disciples that they could do nothing apart from him. In John 16 v 7, Jesus tells his disciples that it is to their advantage that he departs so that the Spirit might come. Paul, in Romans 8 v 13, tells us that only through the power of the Spirit can we put to death "**the deeds of the body.**" The Scriptures everywhere attest to our need for God's Spirit. In Acts 15 the Spirit is mentioned briefly but acts powerfully. He protected the church and guided the apostles and elders. The role of the Spirit, however, does not mean these leaders were passive. On the contrary, the apostles make clear, by co-authoring the letter, their approval of the council's deliberations. The role of the Spirit does not mean that we abdicate our responsibility as disciples of Christ to think and discern. We should not, however, dare to embark on our Christian pilgrimage without the presence of God and a daily dependence upon the Spirit to guide us.

Right Theology and Christian Fellowship

Christian fellowship devoid of sound theology is no true fellowship. Likewise, theology which does not stir up the body of Christ toward fellowship and worship is no true theology. **Verses 30-35** contain the response of the churches to the Jerusalem letter. These verses reveal what happens when the people of God encounter right theology.

Remember, the Gentile Christians have lived with trouble and angst since the disagreement over the law erupted in their region. The Gentile Christians in Antioch await with eagerness a word from the apostles. Finally, Paul and Barnabas return with Judas and Silas. The Antiochene Christians hear the news of Paul's return, and the congregation gathers together to receive the letter of the apostles. Insert yourself into the world of these first-century Christians. We cannot understand the significance of this letter if we fail to empathize with our brothers and sisters of antiquity. There, in a crowded

As they began to read the letter, no doubt an expectant hush blanketed the room.

room in Antioch, new Christians assembled together with a host of emotions flooding their thoughts and minds. The proclamation from the apostles would change their lives and exert a profound effect upon the community. As Judas and Silas began to read the letter, no doubt the air stood still and an expectant hush blanketed the room.

The letter's words pierced the silence and resulted in the praise of the people. They rejoiced at the news and were encouraged by its instruction (**v 31**). The episode in Antioch reveals the inseparable bond between right theology and Christian fellowship. This distillation of the true gospel strengthened the faith and solidified the unity of the Antioch disciples.

Sometimes, Christians might be tempted to think of theology and doctrinal discourse as a hindrance to authentic Christian fellowship. Indeed, many in the church believe that doctrinal matters should not step over the boundaries of the seminaries and theological institutions. Such a sentiment shrugs off matters of theology, fearing that such talk will harden the hearts and minds of believers in a community. Acts 15, however, corrects such concerns and establishes the vital connection between theology and fellowship. As the Holy Spirit protected the church and its doctrine, glorious praise and rejoicing erupted from the teaching of sound theology. Doctrine and theology, when aimed at ushering believers' hearts into greater worship of God, will not harden a congregation; rather, it will strengthen and encourage the faith of the body. Sound teaching of right theology fosters Christ-exalting fellowship.

Judas and Silas remained in Antioch and continued to preach (**v 32**). Luke shows us the power of preaching here. The words of Judas and Silas bore fruit among the congregation and emboldened the Christians in their faith. God established the preaching of his word as the means of strengthening the body of Christ. Indeed, Paul writes in Romans 10 that "faith comes from hearing, and hearing through the word of Christ." The church should not run away from preaching nor view it as an antiquated mode of drawing in new people to a congregation. God makes clear throughout the Scriptures the surpassing power of faithful preaching. Here, in Acts 15, Luke gives us a glimpse of the power of preaching. The words of Judas and Silas, by God's empowerment and grace, nourished the disciples' faith.

After some time in Antioch, the church sent Judas and Silas back to Jerusalem (**v 33**). The section ends with a feeling of great joy and unity. Luke describes the church as sending Judas and Silas off "in peace." Paul and Barnabas remain in Antioch to continue the work of "preaching the word of the Lord" (**v 35**).

A Bitter Departure

The joy and fellowship which permeate the previous verses comes to an abrupt halt in **verses 36-41**. Paul decides, after some time of preaching in Antioch, that he needs to return to the churches he planted on his first missionary journey. In an age before email and social media, Paul had little to no information on the well-being of the churches he had planted. He longed to return to them and strengthen them in their faith and see how they had progressed in discipleship.

Paul asks Barnabas to accompany him (**v 36**). This makes sense given that the elders of Antioch commissioned and set apart both Barnabas and Paul for the missionary task. Barnabas makes a suggestion, however, which leads to a bitter quarrel and argument between himself and Paul.

Back in Acts 13, John Mark had accompanied Paul and Barnabas on their missionary journey. As that mission turned toward Gentile lands, however, Mark deserted the company. Now, two years or so later, Barnabas wants to bring Mark along with them in their second missionary journey (**v 37**). Barnabas again shows the power of

Christian love and forgiveness. If you remember, Barnabas was the first disciple to accept Paul as a brother in Christ. Paul, however, does not want John Mark to join their company (**v 38**). Where Barnabas exudes sympathy and forgiveness, Paul prioritizes the demanding needs of the mission and his vision for the gospel. The divergence leads to a sharp disagreement leading to the separation of these two friends and brothers in the faith (**15:39**).

Is Barnabas or Paul in the right? Luke does not tell us. He makes no judgments. Instead, we can learn valuable principles from this text. First, Christians ought to imitate the kindheartedness and forgiving spirit of Barnabas. Forgiveness flows from a heart which knows it has been forgiven by God. Second, however, we must learn from Paul's conviction and determination. While we must be apt to forgive, we must not let emotional attachments direct our gospel vision. Paul knew the challenges of the road before him and his team, and he did not view Mark as suited for the task. Paul knew the trials that he would face on this journey. He knew the suffering that would come. He needed, therefore, a team of people of proven conviction and determination, who would be ready to die for the gospel.

The real tragedy of this text is not the separation itself but the manner of the separation. There will come a time when gospel laborers need to separate—because of doctrinal difference or even personality issues. Paul and Barnabas could have separated on good terms, still disagreeing, but with a cordial, Christ-honoring attitude. Instead, it seems they left each other in bitterness. Disagreements will come, even to the house of God's people. Christians still inhabit a world of sin and bodies prone to rebellion. We must not be surprised when disagreements come. We must, however, learn from this episode between Paul and Barnabas. Separation in the mission might be the right course of action but it must be done in godliness and in holiness.

Barnabas took Mark with him, no doubt to advance the cause of the gospel in Cyprus (**v 39**). Paul continued on his journey, this time with Silas (**v 40**). They continued throughout Syria and Cilicia "strengthening the churches" (**v 41**). Despite the sharp separation between Paul and Barnabas, neither one of them gave up on the mission or the task to which God had called them.

Questions for reflection

1. Who are some of your heroes of the faith, and how do they encourage you to walk with God?

2. How can you proactively seek to discuss doctrine with other Christians, in a way that strengthens and encourages both them and yourself?

3. Had you been Paul or Barnabas, how do you think you would have handled the disagreement? When disagreements occur, are you ever tempted to be most concerned with maintaining your reputation with friends, or a veneer of peace, or your pride?

3. A CLOTH-DEALER, A SLAVEGIRL, AND A JAILER

Acts 16 provides some of the book's most iconic moments. We meet one of Paul's closest disciples and continue to see the Spirit-filled message of salvation shared with Gentiles. And yet, we also see what great lengths Paul and Timothy go to in order to break down potential barriers to the gospel among the Jews.

Paul's Protégé

Acts **16:1** introduces us to Paul's protégé Timothy. While Paul traveled through Derbe and Lystra, Luke tells us "a disciple was there, named Timothy." Timothy is a significant figure in the life of Paul and his ministry, so we ought to have a working knowledge of who he is. A resident of Lystra, Timothy is described as "the son of a Jewish woman who was a believer, but [whose] father was a Greek." 2 Timothy 1:5 gives us more information about Timothy's family: his mother was Eunice and his grandmother was Lois. Paul most likely had them in mind as the ones who taught Timothy the Scriptures at an early age (2 Timothy 3:14–15). Very little is known of Timothy's father except that he "was a Greek."

Luke also describes Timothy as "a disciple ... well spoken of by the brothers" (Acts **16:2**). This is Luke's typical way of saying that Timothy had a very good reputation among believers. Not only was Timothy a man of good reputation—which, Paul notes, is one of the requirements for a church elder (1 Timothy 3:7); he was also one in whom others saw potential to serve as a leader in the church. Evidently it did not take long to recognize that Timothy was a faithful and gifted brother in the Lord. In writing to Timothy several years later, Paul said, "Do not neglect the gift you have" (1 Timothy 4:14). Timothy was given the gift of prophecy, and he was a preacher. Looking at how the New Testament presents Timothy then, we see a man who had godly character and a good reputation—a young leader full of potential.

With respect to Timothy's age, the book of Acts is silent. Scholars believe Paul wrote 1 Timothy approximately 14 years after their initial meeting. Even then, Paul encourages Timothy to "let no one despise you for your youth" (1 Timothy 4:12). By the best reconstructions, Timothy was either in very late adolescence or young manhood in Acts 16, probably somewhere around the age of 18.

Timothy's Situation

In Acts **16:3**, Luke recounts Paul's desire for Timothy to accompany him on his missionary journey. Timothy, however, on account of his Greek father, has not been circumcised. This situation is more complex than it first appears, and if we pass over it too quickly, we miss one of the supreme ironies in the entire book.

To fully grasp this incident, recall the events surrounding the Jerusalem Council, described in Acts 15. Certain individuals had gone from Jerusalem to Antioch and taught that a Gentile must be circumcised—that is, become a Jew—in order to become a believer in the Lord Jesus Christ. This issue created such a crisis in the young Antiochene church that the Jerusalem Council convened just to rectify it. James resolved the matter by declaring, "We should not trouble those of the Gentiles who turn to God" by requiring circumcision (15:19). In other words, circumcision wasn't obligatory. And yet in Acts 16, Luke makes clear that Paul wants to circumcise Timothy, which, at first glance, seems to oppose the Jerusalem Council.

In order to resolve this apparent discrepancy, we need to remind ourselves of two points. First, the question in Antioch was whether Gentiles should be circumcised in order to be a Christian. Second, Timothy was a Jew because his mother was a Jew, but she had violated the Old Testament law by failing to have her son circumcised. So, the resolution of the Jerusalem Council had no direct bearing on whether Timothy, a Jew, should be circumcised. Paul, however, understood that as long as Timothy remained uncircumcised, his faithfulness to the law, his identity as a Jew, and his spiritual integrity would be questioned. Furthermore, Paul knew that for Timothy to have the kind of authority, respect, and integrity that would be required of him in ministry—especially in ministry to the Jews—he must be circumcised. Timothy's lack of circumcision was a potential stumbling block. It was a hindrance to the gospel, so Paul took Timothy and circumcised him.

To be clear, while circumcision made Timothy more of a Jew, it did not make him any more of a Christian. It did, however, demonstrate his faithfulness as a Christian in undergoing circumcision in order to remove that impediment to his preaching and ministry among the Jews. He was willing to endure the procedure for the sake of the gospel. Only faith can secure salvation. At the same time, some works and acts are wise for evangelism. That continues to be the case today. We are called to be "all things to all people that by all means [we] might save some" (1 Corinthians 9:22). Timothy demonstrated the heart of an **evangelist** and servant of Christ, willing to do whatever it took to see people come to saving faith.

Spirit-Led Mission

Acts **16:4-5** demonstrates how the early church viewed their writings. Paul and his company delivered the "decisions that had been reached" by the Jerusalem Council in chapter 15. These decrees were initially intended for the church at Antioch. But in these verses, we see Paul taking these decrees to the Christians in the cities of Asia Minor, including Derbe, Lystra, and Iconium. In other words, Paul and the early church saw the council's decree as having a two-fold purpose. First, the decree resolved a specific issue in Antioch. And, second, the principles articulated in the decree benefited other churches.

This concept is still relevant to us today. Paul wrote his letters to the Corinthians, for example, to address certain situations within the Corinthian church. The Holy Spirit, however, inspired the Corinthian letters and intended them for the church throughout the ages. Because of the inspiration of the Holy Spirit, we see that God's word not only transcends people groups but also spans thousands of years, thus making it applicable to us today.

> God's word not only transcends people groups but also spans thousands of years.

The benefits of Paul's labors are evident in **16:5** as the churches are strengthened in the faith and grow in number, all on a daily basis. To clarify, when the book of Acts refers to "the faith," it refers to the Christian faith—the message of the gospel and life lived according to it. So, here we see that these early Christians are being confronted with the gospel and being transformed by the power of God. The power of the gospel grows these new converts as disciples of the Lord Jesus Christ.

As Paul, Silas, and Timothy continue their journeys, they travel through the Phrygian and Galatian region and then on to Mysia (**v 6-8**). Here we see that the Holy Spirit prevents them from going to certain parts of Asia or to Bithynia. And yet, starting in **verse 9**, we see the Holy Spirit lead Paul and his company to the next phase of their missionary journey—in Macedonia. In both instances, the Spirit directs Paul's missionary journeys. Despite how such a strategy may have looked to others, Paul and his team faithfully followed the leadership of the Holy Spirit in their ministry endeavors.

This passage marks a significant transition in Paul's missionary journey as well as in the makeup of Paul's missionary team. Luke's use of pronouns changes from "they" to "we". Luke has joined Paul's party. Luke, however, does not tag along as a disinterested journalist or historian. He serves as a fellow member in Paul's missionary team who affirms the mission: "God had called us to preach the gospel to them" (**v 10**).

After much traveling, Paul and his companions arrived in Philippi, a leading city of the area known as Macedonia, and stayed there for some time (**v 12**). On the Sabbath, they "went outside the gate to the riverside" (**v 13**). Why would the Jews gather at a riverside? First, the Roman Empire had previously expelled all of the Jews from Rome in AD 49, which was likely a year before Paul and his party arrived in Philippi. The trickle-down effect of this decision was that while the Roman Empire allowed Jews in places like Philippi, they would not allow them to worship in the city. So, the Jews that wanted to worship would have to go outside the gates of the city. Second, the Jews would usually put a synagogue, if possible, very close to moving water because of the ceremonial washing required to prepare for worship. And where there was no synagogue, they would often gather close to moving water.

Luke indicates again that Paul's missiological method began by preaching first to the Jews. Paul utilized his knowledge of the Jews who gathered for prayer on the Sabbath in order that he could proclaim to them the gospel. Luke records that Paul's primary audience was made up of women. The narrative does not divulge why Jewish women were present without Jewish men. Luke does not concern himself with that question. Rather, he wants to draw our attention to a special event—the **conversion** of Lydia.

Lydia's Conversion

Luke begins to slow down his narrative considerably in **verses 11-15**, particularly as it concerns the conversion of Lydia. When a biblical author starts providing this much detail, he wants to highlight a critical development within the narrative. Lydia runs a business which sells "purple goods" (**v 14**) and is therefore probably a fairly wealthy woman. The color purple denoted royalty. Purple also served to identify an individual as part of the political establishment of the Roman Empire. Purple clothing also indicated wealth.

Not only is Lydia a seller of purple fabrics, but she's also described as a worshiper of God. She's not a Jew; otherwise Luke would have identified her as one. She's a religious Gentile at the river for prayer because she understands and acknowledges Yahweh as the one true and living God. At the riverside, she hears Paul preaching the gospel, and as she does, the Lord "opened her heart" to respond in faith.

Lydia's conversion reminds us of God's sovereignty in the process of salvation. The Lord opens the hearts of sinners to receive the gospel. No one can say they came to the Lord because of their intellect, spiritual sensitivity, or moral uprightness. Rather, as with Lydia, the Lord opens our hearts so we can repent and believe. The Scriptures abound with the saving, gracious work of God, who powerfully opens the eyes of the blind and softens the hearts of the dead (for example, Luke 24:45; Ephesians 1:18). Scripture is also clear that those who hear the gospel have a duty to respond (for example, Acts 2:38; 17:30–31; Romans 10:13), but they will not respond in faith unless the Lord first opens their heart. Lydia hears the gospel, and she responds.

This episode should encourage Christians to faithfully proclaim the gospel with gladness and boldness. As God gave Paul the privilege of leading Lydia to Christ, so too does he give all his people the joy of joining in on his mission to save the lost. God, in his sovereignty, chose his church to serve as his ambassadors. Knowing this should make believers more desirous to speak to nonbelievers, and more committed to pray that God would open their hearts to Jesus' saving power.

Following her conversion, Lydia invites Paul and his companions to come to her house and stay with her. As a result, her household is **baptized** (Acts **16:15**). This does not mean that everybody in Lydia's house was baptized regardless of whether they had made any profession of faith in Christ. This verse, therefore, does not undermine the necessity of belief before baptism. Indeed, the Acts narrative sets out a clear pattern of the gospel preached and the gospel received by faith, followed by the obedience of baptism.

Upon her conversion, Lydia opens her home to Paul. Saved by faith and now unified to Christ, Lydia belongs to the family of God. As such, she displays Christian hospitality and seeks to serve her brothers in Christ. As it was then, so it is now that sacrificial and loving hospitality marks the character of believers in Jesus Christ.

Questions for reflection

1. What are some modern-day examples that reflect the principle we see in Paul circumcising Timothy: that is, of removing impediments for the sake of the gospel?

2. What do you think it looks like to have a life and ministry that is led by the Holy Spirit today?

3. How do the roles of God and of Paul in Lydia's conversion encourage you to speak regularly and boldly of Christ? What will that mean, specifically, in the coming week?

PART TWO

In the next part of this passage, we see the Lord continuing to work in powerful ways through the ministry of the apostles. After working in the heart of Lydia and her household, verses 16-40 show us the Lord at work in the hearts of some very unlikely characters—and using very unlikely means to lead them to saving faith in Jesus Christ.

Good News for One...

In **verse 16**, the scene shifts as Luke introduces a slave girl who has a spirit of divination and is a fortune-teller. We should take careful note of this girl's words in **verse 17**, as they are impeccably accurate, despite coming from such an unlikely source. This slave girl, possessed by an evil spirit, identifies Paul and his team as "servants of the Most High God, who proclaim to you the way of salvation." One of the names the Old Testament uses to identify Yahweh, the God of Israel, is "Most High" (for example, Genesis 14:18–22; Deuteronomy 32:8). We do not know why the slave girl would echo the Old Testament, but Luke tells us that she continued this practice of following Paul and his companions around while shouting out their identity for many days (Acts **16:18**).

Paul did not believe that the shouts of a fortune-teller aided his ministry. Luke tells us that Paul became "greatly annoyed" with her. Paul's message had credibility because it flowed from the authority of Christ. Paul understood that allowing this satanically influenced fortune-teller to make these claims hindered the gospel he proclaimed and the authority by which he ministered. After putting up with this distraction for several days, Paul finally reached his breaking point and commanded the spirit, in the name of Jesus Christ, to come out of the girl. Paul did not ask or invite the demon to come out. Rather, speaking by the authority and power of Jesus, he commanded this demon to leave the girl. Unlike in the kind of drama found in movie scripts, this demon came out of the woman "at that moment" (**v 18**, NIV).

A few additional observations regarding this supernatural encounter are in order. First, **exorcisms** in the New Testament primarily point to the power of God, not the one who performs the exorcism. The power to exorcise demons did not reside in Paul or any other apostle who performed such miracles. Power and authority over the spiritual forces of evil rests in Jesus Christ alone. Second, when demons were cast out in the New Testament, that person concerned received spiritual healing as well as physical healing. In other words, such people experienced complete healing, which includes freedom from demon possession and a new redeemed relationship with God. Indeed, Jesus himself pointed out that exorcism remains useless unless the indwelling of God replaces the indwelling of evil (Luke 11:20-26). This girl not only received deliverance from the evil spirit, but she also came to saving knowledge and faith in Jesus Christ.

Bad News for Others

While the healing of this young woman was good news to her personally, Luke shows us that it was bad news for others. In the following verses, Luke reports, "But when her owners saw that their hope of gain was gone, they seized Paul and Silas and dragged them into the marketplace before the rulers. And when they had brought them to the magistrates, they said, 'These men are Jews, and they are disturbing our city. They advocate customs that are not lawful for us as Romans to accept or practice'" (Acts **16:19-21**). This miraculous healing spelled financial disaster for the girl's masters because her fortune-telling ability had come to an end. Upon realizing that their monetary hope had been dashed, the owners of the girl seized Paul and Silas, and dragged them into the marketplace for an immediate hearing before the local magistrates. The marketplace functioned as a gathering place for all types of trade and as a place for the local rulers or magistrates to hear and resolve disputes.

Paul's accusers charged him with "disturbing our city" by promoting "customs that are not lawful for us as Romans to accept or practice" (**v 20–21**). Before proceeding, there are two quick historical observations that need to be addressed. First, Jews had been expelled from Rome. Judaism, however, still enjoyed legal status throughout the Roman Empire, though **proselytizing** remained unlawful. Second, the Roman authorities saw little to no distinction between Judaism and Christianity. At this point in church history, Christianity was seen as a subset of Judaism. Tying these two points together, we now see that the Christians were breaking the law by their evangelism. With these points framing the context, we can understand why the accusers do not mention their slave girl or her exorcism. They assert, rather, that Paul and Silas present a threat to civil stability and need to be dealt with swiftly. Seeing the gathered crowd turning into a mob, the magistrates ordered Paul and Silas to be stripped and beaten with rods (**v 22**) and then thrown into prison (**v 23-24**).

Paul and Silas in Prison

In the Roman Empire, a prison not only housed convicted criminals but also held individuals awaiting their impending judgment. Although an initial judgment (the beating) has occurred, the fact that Paul and Silas have been thrown into prison implies that more judgment is coming. Such judgment could entail exile, additional beatings, or execution. Since Paul and Silas are accused of trying to subvert the Roman Empire by means of sharing the gospel, the consequence would likely be capital punishment. And yet, at this precise moment, a remarkable turn of events occurs.

Paul and Silas spent their time in prison praying and singing hymns to God (**v 25**). Their surprising response to imprisonment flowed from their steadfast trust in the sovereign hand of God. They could worship in prison because they knew that, whether free or in shackles, they belonged to the God of the universe. As they sang and prayed, a divine earthquake shook the foundations of the prison, opened its doors, and unfastened everyone's chains (**v 25–26**). Following such a supernatural event, the next thing we might logically expect would be for the prisoners to leave the prison. The jailer assumes this has occurred and prepares to kill himself because the punishment for letting prisoners escape is death (**v 27**). At this moment, Paul cries out, urging the jailer to lay down his sword and not harm himself, because the unthinkable has occurred—all the prisoners have remained in prison (**v 28**). The jailer recognizes the supernatural nature of the earthquake. He also realizes the uniqueness of Paul and Silas as prisoners, as evidenced by their praying and singing. The jailer cannot comprehend the type of character Paul, Silas, and the other prisoners have exuded by staying in the cells (**v 29**). While the jailer is relieved to know no prisoner has escaped, he also understands that something inexplicable has occurred.

> Here is one of the most important questions asked in the New Testament.

This scene sets the stage for one of the most important questions asked in the New Testament. The jailer undoubtedly understood that Paul and Silas were in jail because of a riot caused, at least in part, because they had been identified as "servants of the Most High God" who were preaching "the way of salvation" (**v 17**). The jailer also knew that, unlike other prisoners, they were singing and praising God despite having suffered a horrendous beating. Hence, the Lord used the faithfulness of Paul and Silas in the face of their suffering so that the gain a hearing from the jailer. Following their imprisonment, a miraculous earthquake had opened the prison doors and unfastened their chains. There was no other explanation. And so the jailer immediately cut to the chase with razor-like focus to his question: "Sirs, what must I do to be saved" (**v 30**)?

The behavior of Paul and Silas in the midst of difficulty provided a powerful testimony for the jailer. He fell to the ground and asked for the way of salvation because he had seen God in Paul and Silas.

He had seen the power of the Lord manifested through them and around him. How often do Christians today find themselves asked questions about the way of salvation? Perhaps many Christians today fail to exhibit the joy of the gospel in the midst of trials, as Paul and Silas did that night. Perhaps believers in Christ today surrender their godliness and do not exude the fruit of the Spirit, as Paul and Silas had throughout their time in Philippi. Like moths drawn to a flame, nonbelievers will often run toward the light of Christ as he manifests himself through those who faithfully walk in accordance with his ways. Let us be those who live that kind of witness, that we might also have the opportunity to witness to Christ with our words.

The Way of Salvation

The way a person answers the jailer's question demonstrates their entire understanding of the gospel. Moreover, everything a person understands about the gospel, Jesus Christ, sin, and salvation comes down to how a person answers the jailer's question.

With his customary precision, Paul succinctly answers the jailer in **verse 31**: "Believe in the Lord Jesus, and you will be saved, you and your household." The belief Paul speaks about rises above thinking the right thoughts about Jesus. The type of belief Paul has in mind requires an element of active trust which relies on Christ's accomplished work. For Paul, this type of belief is intellectual in nature. A person cannot rely on Christ and turn from sin without a minimum of intellectual understanding of the truth about the gospel and the nature of Jesus. Intellectual assent, however, will not produce salvation. Saving faith also involves the will. A person's will must be engaged and respond to the gospel, in faith, for that person to be saved.

Paul's statement is so foundational that two additional comments are in order before leaving it. First, Paul does not say, "You might be saved." Rather, he confidently declares, "You will be saved." Inspired by the Holy Spirit, Paul's declaration announces the positive, unconditional promise of salvation based upon the gift of faith.

Second, Paul's closing phrase—"you and your household"—raises questions that must be addressed. In the book of Acts, when a person comes to a saving knowledge of Jesus Christ and faith in him, their family will often follow (for example, Cornelius in Acts 10). The faith of one family member, however, never saves another individual from their sins. Their testimony and life, however, provide a glorious opportunity for the gospel in households. As fathers and mothers love their children through the teaching of the gospel and display the sublime virtues of Christian living, children may, by God's grace, come to saving faith—and God is often pleased to work in this way. In Acts 16, **verse 32** sheds some light on this issue. Paul and Silas "spoke the word of the Lord [the gospel] to him and to all who were in his house." The jailer's household, therefore, came to saving faith because the jailer had brought Paul and Silas to his house, where they preached the gospel, which transformed hearts (see Romans 10:13-17). Luke tells us in Acts **16:33** that the jailer and his household followed their **professions of faith** with baptism to demonstrate their changed lives and decision to follow Christ. Further evidence of their changed lives is seen in the way the jailer and his household washed and cared for Paul and Silas (**v 33-34**).

An Unlikely Church

With dawn, a time of critical testing arrived (**v 35-37**). At some point during the night, the jailer had brought Paul and Silas back to the jail, as he didn't have the authority to release them. The magistrates sent their police to the prison, ordering the release of Paul and Silas. The magistrates had evidently decided they were going to release these men and send them on their way, since it was more politically expedient to release them than to give them the publicity of a trial. In response to the directive to leave, Paul responds, "They have beaten us publicly, uncondemned, men who are **Roman citizens**, and have thrown us into prison; and do they now throw us out secretly? No! Let them come themselves and take us out" (**v 37**).

Roman citizenship was beyond any kind of monetary value in the ancient world. Indeed, the authorities showed great respect for Paul and Silas' status (**v 38-39**). They even apologized to them. Paul leveraged his status as a Roman citizen, with all the privileges that went with it, in order to go about his mission of preaching the gospel to the ends of the earth. Paul's example calls all Christians to **steward** their privileges toward the glory of God and for **kingdom work**. Upon their release, Paul and Silas continued to demonstrate their unwavering commitment to serving others by encouraging their new converts and their brothers and sisters in the faith (**v 40**).

The chapter concludes with the departure of Paul and Silas. They leave behind, however, an unlikely band of disciples. There, in Philippi, the church comprised, among others, a rich businesswoman, an ex-slave girl, and a Gentile jailer. In this scene, the gospel triumphed as it brought together people from all walks of life into an unshakeable unity sealed by the blood of Christ. This was a blood-bought people who now, by their common faith in Christ, had become eternal brothers and sisters.

Questions for reflection

1. Christianity was perceived as a subversion of Roman culture (v 20-24). In what ways is Christianity perceived to be a threat to your society's culture today?

2. Paul's response to suffering drew the jailer to ask him about salvation. In what way are you walking through trials right now? Who might be watching how you handle them? How might they be the means of giving you opportunities to share the gospel?

3. Is your heart's desire to be able to tell people around you what Paul told the jailer? Why / why not? What do you need to pray about?

4. THIS I PROCLAIM TO YOU

Acts 17 contains some of Paul's most powerful and well-known sermons. He delivers the gospel to Jews but also to Gentiles. Paul knows the gospel can powerfully save Jews and Gentiles alike. Indeed, as Paul wrote in Romans 1:16, "I am not ashamed of the gospel, for it is the power of God for salvation to everyone who believes, to the Jew first and also to the Greek." Paul, however, contextualizes his message in Acts 17 depending on his audience. In so doing, he demonstrates the versatility of the gospel as one message of truth which can reach entirely different cultures.

Into Thessalonica

God called Paul to go to Macedonia to preach the gospel (16:9-10). When Paul and Silas arrived in the region, they visited Philippi (v 12), Amphipolis, Apollonia, and Thessalonica (**17:1**). Knowing the geography and history of that region is important for Christians to better understand the background of Acts 17.

Amphipolis was situated between rivers flowing to the southwest in Macedonia, while Thessalonica was located in the southwest region. Thessalonica became a famous city in the ancient world as a result of controversies involving its territory and military activities. It was used as a base by the military forces of Pompey "the Great" during his civil war with Julius Caesar in 49-48BC (Caesar would defeat Pompey before going on to assume the role of emperor).

Thessalonica became not only a business-friendly economic environment and a **free city**, but also a city of refuge for the Jews after their expulsion from Rome sixteen years previously. Jews had sought another city that resembled Rome, and Thessalonica came to be that hospitable place. When Paul and Silas arrived in Thessalonica, they went to a synagogue (**v 1**). Synagogues continued to serve as crucial priorities and targets in Paul's missionary strategy.

He Had to Die

On three Sabbaths, Paul reasoned with the Jews from the Scriptures (**v 2**). He did not present the message of the gospel through a philosophical argument or any eloquent **oratory**. Paul grounded his faith in the message of the gospel itself and the power of the Scriptures to change hardened hearts. He also knew that in the Old Testament Scriptures he had common ground with the Jews upon which to build his message.

From the Scriptures, Paul reasoned with the Jews in the synagogue by giving evidence, arguments, and reasonable explanations for the claim that Jesus was the Christ (**v 3**). That message was a **stumbling block** for the Jews (1 Corinthians 1:23). For them, the Messiah would come to release Jews from Roman oppression, and he would establish a new nationalistic state. To accomplish these goals, they believed that the Christ would rise up as a king and a military leader. Thus, claiming that Jesus—who died on a Roman cross instead of conquering Rome—was the Messiah offended the Jewish **worldview**.

Paul, however, did not give an inch. He continued preaching that Jesus was in fact the Christ (Acts **17:3**). If the Jews had understood the Scriptures as Paul did, they would have expected that the Messiah was going to be the servant of the Lord who would come, be rejected by men, be pierced for their **transgressions**, be crushed by God, pour out his soul to death, and, by his wounds, heal his people (Isaiah 53:3, 5, 10, 12).

The Messiah, therefore, had to die. Indeed, the Messiah did die on a Roman cross. Jesus Christ of Nazareth hung on a **tree** and bled and died for the sins of his people. That was Paul's Messiah, and that was the gospel he proclaimed. The triune God, in his own character, cannot tolerate sin. God would cease to be God if he did not execute judgment against sin. Someone had to pay the price. Either Christ has borne our penalty on the cross, or we will bear it ourselves in eternity.

Conversion and Opposition

After Paul's preaching, some of the Jews came to Christ, as well as many Greeks who were Jewish converts, and "not a few of the leading women" (Acts **17:4**). Paul's presentation of the gospel, therefore, had had a powerful effect on the crowd. Some Jews became jealous and opposed the response to Paul's message. The Jews hatched a plot to stir up wicked men from the marketplace into a mob. The mob set the city in an uproar and started a riot (**v 5**). Thessalonica boasted 200,000 residents. That was no small city. The chaos could have rapidly escalated out of control and engulfed the entire city in violence. This would have caused enormous problems for the civic leaders. Failure to subdue the mob would have led to a judgment of incompetence and inability to govern from the authorities and powers in Rome. The local leaders, therefore, needed to end the revolt lest they be deposed.

In the Gospels, Pontius Pilate was caught in a similar dilemma, in which he had the option of either listening to the Jews and the crowds, and crucifying Jesus, or going against their will and negating their request. That could have led to an uproar and rebellion; and Pilate would have been held responsible and seen as incapable of governing Jerusalem. For one of the main tasks of a governor was to keep his province quiet and obedient to the Roman Empire. Insurrections were met with strong and violent responses.

Here, the mob targets the house of Jason (**v 5**). Probably Jason was a wealthy believer who offered his house as a refuge for Paul and Silas, and for church meetings. It is crucial to notice that in early Christianity, there were no church buildings for believers to meet in. Because of that, believers had to meet in houses. Those who had bigger homes could practice hospitality by hosting church meetings; and that seems to have been the case with Jason. The mob, therefore, headed straight for the house of the man who housed the Christians.

Notice the three-fold pattern: first, Paul preaches; second, the gospel advances; third, the message elicits a response. While some turn from their sins and believe Christ, others oppose it. Whenever the gospel spreads, it will provoke a response. A person cannot answer with neutrality when presented with the message of Christ. Either nonbelievers will repent or they will turn away. Often, the rejection can turn hostile, which happens here in Acts 17. When the gospel collides with unbelief, it will spark flames of discord and controversy.

Turning the World Upside Down

As soon as the mob reached Jason's house, they tried to find Paul and Silas—but both of them were absent (**v 6**). Then, the mob dragged Jason and other believers before the city authorities, bringing three charges against them.

First, they accused the Christians as those who had "turned the world upside down." Second, they accused Jason of being hospitable toward Paul and Barnabas—who, they claimed, were acting contrary to the decrees of Caesar (**v 7**). Third, the mob charged the Christians with proclaiming the rule of another king named Jesus. To all three counts, I hope every Christian would say, "Guilty as charged!"

The mob "hit the nail on the head". Christians should turn the world upside down. Christians do love their fellow believers and serve them so that the cause of the gospel might expand. Christians must proclaim, not even another king, but the King of kings and Lord of lords. That is exactly what Christians do when they faithfully proclaim the gospel.

Conversely, we see so many churches today that have relinquished the gospel and doctrinal fidelity. Instead, they serve the cultural whims and alter the core tenets of the faith in order to modernize it in keeping with the times. A plethora of churches today have signed up for the cultural and moral revolution that has swept through Western societies in the past sixty years or so, committing high treason against the King of the cosmos. When a church denies the sole kingship of Christ, it is no longer a church. When Christians try to blend into the flow of the culture rather than turn it upside down with the gospel, they no longer practice faithfulness. Faithful Christians disrupt because they carry a message which pierces hearts and offends corrupt minds. When Christians faithfully proclaim the gospel, they seek to dismantle Satan's hold on the world. Make no mistake, gospel preaching will turn the world upside down, and that is glorious.

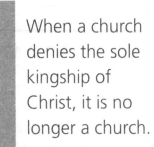

When a church denies the sole kingship of Christ, it is no longer a church.

As a result of the charges and the dramatic situation, the city authorities became disturbed and interrogated the believers (**v 8**). Probably, they could see no advantage in imprisoning the believers, so they preferred to take a bond from Jason and the others. After that all of the believers were released (**v 9**).

Paul and Silas in Berea

"The brothers immediately sent Paul and Silas away by night to Berea" (**v 10**). The Christians in Thessalonica hoped to spare Paul and Silas any more violence in the city. They thought it best to send them away and to let things calm down in the city. Had Paul and Silas stayed, the Jews may have incited another mob which could have harmed or even killed the apostles. Out of a concern for their safety, they sent them away to Berea.

As soon as Paul and Silas arrived in Berea, they did not miss a beat but went into the synagogue to preach the gospel (**v 10**). The plethora of synagogues in the region stems from Caesar's expulsion of the Jews from Rome in AD 49. Jews had to find new homes throughout the Roman Empire. Wherever they settled, they would establish a synagogue for the teaching of their faith and the preservation of their culture. Paul utilized these synagogues as natural places where he could share the gospel. In the same way, Christians might be surprised by the number of places where natural gospel conversations can take place. Christians can steward simple conversations toward spiritual matters. When we get our hair cut, when we chat with coworkers, or when we see our neighbors, God has orchestrated a multitude of opportunities for us to share the gospel.

Faith Found, Mob Follows

Luke describes the Jews in Berea as nobler than those in Thessalonica (**v 11**). When the Bereans heard Paul's message, they responded with eagerness and examined the Scriptures daily to confirm the validity of the apostle's message. As a result of that examination many believed, "with not a few Greek women of high standing as well as men" (**v 12**).

Preachers of the word must rightly handle the word of truth (2 Timothy 2:15). That is their solemn and prime responsibility. The congregation, however, must test the words of the preacher and ensure that the message does indeed accord with God's revelation and will. The Berean community heard Paul's message, searched the Scriptures, and, by God's grace, came to see the truth of the gospel that Paul proclaimed. They came to a saving faith because they heard the gospel and, with humble hearts, sought to understand its claims. The Christian faith is not a blind faith. The Bible makes claims that require deep contemplation. Indeed, the Bible lays claim to an absolute authority and asserts one way to eternal life. Faith, therefore, must not be seen as "jumping off the cliff." Instead, we come to understand, by God's grace, the truth claims of the Scriptures and place our faith in the well-reasoned, well-articulated power of the gospel.

While Paul had much success in Berea, the Jews from Thessalonica followed him and found him in Berea (Acts **17:13**). They attempted to agitate the people and, in all likelihood, were aiming to stir up another mob to try and kill Paul. As the brothers had in Thessalonica, the Berean Christians smuggled Paul out of the city, sending him away (**v 14**). Luke records that Silas and Timothy remained in the city while Paul proceeded to Athens (**v 15**).

Questions for reflection

1. Paul "reasoned" with the Jews by giving evidence and arguments for the truth of the gospel. Are you able to do the same? What steps could you take to further improve your ability to do so?

2. Consider the accusations made against Jason (on page 62). Would you be found "guilty as charged" regarding each of them? If not, what needs to change?

3. To what extent are you like the Bereans?

PART TWO

Provoked to Witness

Paul now finds himself in Athens, where he waits for Timothy and Silas. Luke writes, "Now while Paul was waiting for them at Athens, his spirit was provoked within him as he saw that the city was full of idols" (**v 16**). Paul's soul reacts to his surroundings. He looks around the city with disgust, contempt, and, no doubt, hatred. There in Athens, the people had erected idols with their own hands and bowed down to them as gods. They served carved images rather than the one true God. They worshiped the creature rather than the Creator. Provoked by what he sees, Paul begins to share the gospel.

Do you experience the same kind of provocation when you see people around you serving a false god? What Paul saw were eternal souls worshiping something that could not save. Moreover, he witnessed God's creatures failing to worship God. God alone is worthy of worship. God alone deserves our praise (Exodus 20:2-3; Psalm 145:3). Paul saw his fellow humans rendering worship and ascribing glory to man-made objects. Paul, therefore, proceeds to preach the gospel so that people might practice true worship and God might not be robbed of the glory due to his name.

Christians must adopt the same heart and mindset as Paul. Too often, Christians apathetically look at the world around them and see people worshiping idols. Outrage does not fill the hearts of Christians as they see the name of God defamed and glory given to something other than Yahweh. Indifference has replaced zeal, and lethargy has drowned passion. When God's people see idols worshiped, a righteous anger should burn within their soul. With the blast of a trumpet, the Christian must charge into the battle, storm the gates of the enemy, obliterate the idol, and bring the captives to see the only One worthy of worship.

Repeating his customary evangelistic practice, Paul went to a synagogue and reasoned from Scripture with Jews and God-fearing

Greeks. In addition to visiting the synagogue, Paul went to the crowds in the marketplace (Acts **17:17**), where business as well as social interactions were conducted. The marketplace served as Athens' place of meeting.

Among the people there were some Epicurean and Stoic philosophers. Epicureans believed that the gods had no interest in or influence on the affairs of men. The gods, therefore, had removed themselves from the world. The Stoics, however, believed that everything that happened was determined by a supreme god or organizing principle, which they sometimes identified with the world itself. The Epicureans tended to see life as a matter of open chance, while the Stoics viewed the world through a lens of fatalism. Those promoting each of these competing worldviews heard Paul and said, "What does this babbler wish to say?" Others said, "He seems to be a preacher of foreign divinities" (**v 18**). These thinkers of Athens appeared to be confused and dismissive. Their tone indicates a sense of ridicule. The reason for this comes from Paul's preaching of a resurrection from the dead. Stoic philosophers held the body and the physical world in contempt. They viewed the physical realm as evil and something that people must overcome. Greek philosophy venerated the spiritual realm and saw the spiritual world as something that could only be seen after one had cut oneself off from the physical world. Thus, for Paul to preach a resurrection from the dead did not seem like good news at all.

Greek Philosophy and Western Culture

The talk of Greek philosophy may seem out of place and bear little to no significance for the church today. This kind of philosophy, however, exists today in many forms, even within the Christian faith. It is a belief which denies the goodness of creation and the dignity of the body. It rejects that God made the world good. This kind of thinking has influenced some kinds of Christian spirituality and Christian living. For example, the phrase, "Let go and let God" has become a popular expression among many Christians. That phrase, however, has its roots in the pagan philosophy Paul encountered in Athens. "Let go and let God" is intended to lead people to a **nirvana**-type state of tranquility where they seek to ignore the physical world and, like a jellyfish, float along in their trust for God. True Christian spirituality, however, develops a trust in God through active spiritual disciplines—through daily Bible-reading, prayer, fellowship, and the fight against sin.

The modern **prosperity gospel** also abides by this pagan philosophy with the phrase "Name it and claim it!" In essence, it teaches that if you will your mind to think positively, nothing can stand in your way. You can overcome your cancer diagnosis through a step-by-step spiritual journey. Once you have completed the necessary tasks, God will be on your side and will bless you and heal you.

> God has willed to move through the prayers of his church.

The gospel also confronts the Stoic philosophy of fatalism, which still runs rampant in modernity. Fatalism would say, "Whatever will be, will be." This mindset, however, runs contrary to the biblical notion of responsibility. God has indeed orchestrated all events and works everything according to the counsel of his will (Ephesians 1:11). God's sovereignty, however, does not diminish human responsibility. God works, moves, and brings his plan to completion through the faithful acts of obedience of his people. God has willed to move through the prayers of his church. The gospel unites God's sovereignty and human responsibility in a resplendent mystery. The world is not simply left to fate. The world rests in the hands of God, who moves and acts through the people he has made as they seek to obey, or in some cases, disobey his will.

The pagan philosophies Paul encountered still permeate the thoughts of many today, and even the thoughts of many Christians. Believers, therefore, need constant instruction from the infallible and inerrant word of God. True Christian doctrine does not deny the beauty of the physical. Indeed, we await a new heaven and a new earth. Christians hope for new, perfect, sinless bodies. We affirm the glory of the physical world because God made it, and he made it good. When Christ ushers in the new kingdom, his people will inhabit a physical world, with physical bodies, and it will be more than good. Indeed, it will be perfect.

After Paul's initial interaction with the philosophers in the marketplace, they brought Paul to the Areopagus (Acts **17:19**). The Areopagus, or Mars Hill, was the high point in Athens: the place where thinkers met and where the great temples were. Their curiosity to hear Paul's new teaching and message was evident. They desired to understand new ideas, for they viewed themselves as intellectuals (**v 21**). Instead of calling the apostle an idle babbler, the Athenians were curious. They told Paul, "You bring some strange things to our ears. We wish to know therefore what these things mean" (**v 20**). Their curiosity and intellectual passion turned their ears to Paul and to the message of the gospel.

Paul's Proclamation in the Areopagus

Paul accepted their invitation and stood in the midst of the Areopagus. He said, "Men of Athens, I perceive that in every way you are very religious" (**v 22**). These words might initially appear to be a compliment for their religiosity, but in the context Paul meant something different. He says, "For as I passed along and observed the objects of your worship, I found also an altar with this inscription: 'To the unknown god.' What therefore you worship as unknown, this I proclaim to you" (**v 23**).

First, Paul depersonalized their worship by not calling the objects of their worship "gods" but referring to them as "objects," because they were no deities at all. Second, he asserted their ignorance of the true God. Lastly, with boldness and audacity, Paul punctured their intellectual pomposity and exposed their lack of the knowledge of the truth.

Paul told the Athenians that the God who made the world and everything in it is the "Lord of heaven and earth" (**v 24**), and he is not limited to one location as it was believed by many in the ancient Near East. Do not miss the importance of the doctrine of creation in Paul's theology. Indeed, in **verse 26**, Paul proclaims that God "made from one man every nation of mankind to live on all the face of the earth…" Paul guards and announces the historicity of Adam. Many Christians today willingly surrender the doctrine of creation to sup- posedly irrefutable scientific evidence. For Paul, however, the doctrine of creation, and God's sovereign hand in the act of creation, remains a central pillar of the entire gospel message.

In addition, the biblical God is not "served by human hands" (**v 25**). The reverse is true: contrary to the thought of the Athenian intellectu- als, they needed God for everything. Their hearts beat and their lungs absorbed oxygen because of God's grace. God lacks nothing, nor does he need the service of our hands.

Paul announces in **verse 27** that all humanity should seek after God. God has revealed himself to all mankind through his creation. In- deed, as Paul wrote in Romans 1:20, "his invisible attributes, namely, his eternal power and divine nature, have been clearly perceived, ever since the creation of the world, in the things that have been made. So [people] are without excuse." Consequently, even pagan thinkers are able to grasp some of the divine truth in nature.

Paul, in the midst of his gospel proclamation, does something as- tounding. First, recognize that he has not, at any point, mentioned Jesus Christ or the Messiah. He has not quoted the Old Testament or, as he so often did, reasoned from the Scriptures that the Messiah has come. Paul knew his audience. Consequently, he contextualized his gospel presentation. Paul's missiology does not hold to a rigid format and style of communication for the gospel. When Paul spoke to Jews, he began with the Hebrew Scriptures and moved to their fulfillment in Jesus Christ. Had Paul adopted the same method at Mars Hill, how- ever, he would have lost his audience. These philosophers would have had little to no understanding of the Jewish heritage and tradition.

The second thing Paul does is surprising. In Acts **17:28**, Paul quotes from a pagan poet in order to build his point and illustrate the sovereign creative power of God. Paul probably quotes from Epimenides of Crete and Arastus. The lines Paul quotes would have likely been written about Zeus, the primary pagan god of Greek mythology. Paul borrows from the Athenian culture and utilizes the gems of truth embedded even within their pagan lore. He is driving towards his conclusion in **verse 29**: that since we are made by God, in his image, we must not think that we can create an image and call it God.

This may make some Christians feel uncomfortable. After all, would it not have been better for Paul to quote from the Scriptures? First, remember that at this point the New Testament had not been written. Second, while Paul could have quoted from the Old Testament, he approached his audience on their own ground, on their own turf. He used what would have been familiar from their own worldview in order to build a bridge that connected the message of the gospel to their pagan mindset. Paul contextualized his method in order that the gospel might break through to these particular people. In essence, Paul does not want anything to hinder the gospel from reaching the hearts and minds of his audience. The gospel should be the only stumbling block, not our presentation of the gospel.

True Doctrine Must Be Packaged Wisely

Paul's strategy provides Christians with valuable lessons on evangelism and missions. Christians cannot surrender the theological and doctrinal core of the gospel. Without true doctrine, we have no good news to proclaim. At the same time, Paul shows that we can maintain the truth of the gospel, while packaging our message to meet the needs of a particular audience. A sermon that preaches the gospel to a country church in the middle of the American South will bear little resemblance to a talk that preaches the Scriptures in Zimbabwe. Though both preachers proclaim the same gospel, they do so within their own cultural contexts and according to their customs.

They contextualize the message so that the gospel breaks into that specific culture and worldview.

Acts 17 shows us how we can turn almost every situation or every context into a gospel opportunity. Paul even found within pagan poetry truths about God and the gospel. He used these truths as pillars upon which to build the rest of his gospel presentation. Christians today need to observe the world around them and see the truths of God embedded within their culture and society. All humanity, even though lost in sin, bears the image of God. People's actions, motives, ethics, and desires in some way will point to the God who made them and who longs to redeem them. Find that common ground and use it to share the gospel.

> Acts 17 shows us how we can turn almost every situation into a gospel opportunity.

In **verse 30**, Paul says that "the times of ignorance God overlooked." Paul does not mean that God overlooked sin as if it did not happen or with a sense of neutrality. Sin had not gone unnoticed by God. This verse means that God, by his mercy, had not brought down his wrath or judgment upon these philosophers… yet. God exercised mercy over the sins of the people. Now, however, the time of ignorance has ceased. Jesus Christ has come. Paul now stands as a herald of the gospel message and proclaims the way of salvation. God will not meet this rejection with mercy but with judgment.

Paul concludes his sermon with a call to repentance and the pronouncement of a future day of judgment, with a man resurrected from the dead acting as judge (**v 30-31**). Indeed, Paul grounds the promise of a future day of judgment in the resurrection of Christ. The raising of Jesus from the dead established and proved a future day of judgment. Even in his contextualized message, Paul still calls people to repent. Though he does not mention Jesus, he points to their sin and the need they have for repentance. When Paul mentions the resurrection from the dead, as could be expected, the audience reacts (**v 32-33**).

Again, Paul had contextualized the message, but he would not leave out the central truths of the gospel. He would not surrender doctrine for the sake of popularity. He knew they would not respond well to the idea of resurrection, but Paul could not omit this vital component of the Christian faith. Still, Paul's message had a powerful impact on the audience. The contextualization worked on some who wanted to hear more of Paul. Indeed, some even repented of their sins and became disciples of Jesus Christ (**v 34**).

This chapter concludes with three different responses to the gospel message. Paul met mockery, interest, and conversions. Likewise, Christians today will meet similar responses. Rejections of the message of the gospel by some can stop Christians hoping that others will show true interest and be converted. Although Paul's message was rejected, and some of these rejections turned quite hostile, he also saw interest and glorious conversions throughout his mission. Believers today, therefore, must not let rejections veil their ability to see the work of God. Press on through rejection, continue to share the gospel, and know that God is always with you.

Questions for reflection

1. What are the main idols being worshiped in your culture, and to what extent is your response to that idol-worship the same as Paul's was in Athens?

2. In what ways are you listening to the "poets" and "prophets" of your culture, so that you are best able to explain the gospel in a way that is clear and compelling to those around you?

3. How do verses 32-34 give us a realistic and hopeful expectation of what will happen as we share the gospel?

5. I HAVE MANY IN THIS CITY

Paul's journey progresses to the city of Corinth, a crossroads between east and west (**18:1**). Corinth was on an **isthmus** and had ports on both the east and west sides of the city. Thus, travelers would come from all sides of the Mediterranean, including North Africa. Corinth became a center of economic and political influence. Presumably, this is why Paul only spent a few weeks in Athens but more than a year in Corinth on this second missionary journey (**v 11**). Paul desired to spend time evangelizing and discipling Christians in this city of influence.

The letters of 1 and 2 Corinthians provide more context for Paul's ministry detailed here in Acts 18. One of Paul's primary concerns for the church was the rampant sexual sins found among its members (1 Corinthians 5:1-13; 6:12-20). But these sins should not surprise us, for the city of Corinth was also known as a center of immorality. Corinth was a city dedicated to the Greek goddess, Aphrodite. She reigned as the goddess of love. But Corinth understood love as the practice of virtually any form of sexual immorality. Corinth, therefore, knew how to worship—the city worshiped sexual perversion.

This is important to note for understanding Paul's ministry in Corinth. When Paul proclaimed the truth and grace of the gospel, he attacked two foundations in Corinth. First, he dismantled the **pluralistic** worldview of religion that dominated Greek thinking. Paul preached the oneness of God—monotheism. Second, Paul called for the citizens of Corinth to turn away from their sexual immorality and pursue the Lord (1 Corinthians 6:19-20). Christians, therefore, cannot have one foot in God's kingdom and another in the kingdom of the world.

Luke continues to provide more details about Paul's ministry in Corinth. He met a remarkable couple, Priscilla and Aquila (Acts **18:2**). They were Jews who at one point had lived in Rome but were ejected by **Claudius**. They then moved to Italy and finally reached Corinth, where they were able to start a business. They, like Paul, were tent-makers (**v 3**). We have every reason to believe that Priscilla and Aquila were already believers at this point because Luke does not record their conversion stories. Furthermore, later on in this chapter, Priscilla and Aquila correct the theology of **Apollos** (**v 26**).

Paul moved in with Priscilla and Aquila and worked with them (**v 3**) while proclaiming the gospel in the synagogue as persuasively as he could, seeking to draw both Jews and God-fearing Greeks to faith in Christ (**v 4**).

The tentmakers in the ancient world had a diversity of clients. Shepherds would use tents as they traveled with their animals. As they reached a pasture, the shepherd would set up his tent until the next morning. Also, the military would purchase tents to establish a military camp. Normally, only those of high rank would reside in one in the camp. Furthermore, any traveler could use a tent after reaching the port in Corinth. Tentmakers were always popular in a busy city like Corinth.

Why would Paul labor as a tentmaker? Paul certainly believed that preachers of the gospel deserved wages (1 Corinthians 9:14; 1 Timothy 5:18). Taking time to make and repair tents would have meant Paul did not spend every minute he had preaching the gospel and evangelizing the lost. Paul demonstrates a profound wisdom in making tents. Indeed, he tells us in another letter why he labored as a tentmaker even though he believed gospel preachers deserved a wage. In 1 Thessalonians 2:9, Paul writes, "You remember, brothers, our labor and toil; we worked night and day, that we might not be a burden to any of you, while we proclaimed to you the gospel of God." Furthermore, in 1 Corinthians 9:18, Paul makes clear why, specifically in Corinth, he made tents, writing, "What then is my reward? That in my preaching I may present the gospel free of charge, so as not to make full use of my right in the gospel." Paul worked, therefore, to avoid burdening anyone while he preached, and because he did not want the Corinthians to think he peddled the gospel for the purpose of financial gain. He wanted no hindrance to the work of the gospel. Paul understood his tentmaking as a vital part of his overall ministry.

The Watchman in Corinth

After Paul had been working with Priscilla and Aquila for some time, his companions arrived (**Acts 18:5**). Paul and Silas were visiting the Macedonian churches (17:15) most likely in order to raise support for Paul's ministry. Thus, as they arrive with the churches' contributions, Paul is able to hand the whole tentmaking business back to Priscilla and Aquila and devote himself completely to preaching.

Paul's missiological method in Corinth is similar to the one he used in the many other cities in which he evangelized. He seems to always begin in the synagogue, preaching that Jesus is the Messiah (**18:5**). Paul's message was clear, simple, and cross-centered. How do we know this? Paul detailed what he preached in Corinth, to both the Jews and the Greeks, in 1 Corinthians 2:1-5. He writes that he did not preach with "lofty speech or wisdom" but preached "Jesus Christ and him crucified."

The reaction to Paul's message of the crucified Christ was opposition and anger (Acts **18:6**). This opposition was aimed not only at Paul, but also Christ. It was the message of Christ as the Messiah that caused Jews to revile him. Paul understood this rejection as not an attack on himself but on Jesus. Thus, Paul's reaction was to shake his garments and move on (**v 6**). He did not try to defend himself or his argument. Paul knew the offensive nature of the gospel for proud, hardened hearts.

Paul's response to the rejection is twofold. First, in a symbolic act, Paul shakes out his garment. This is an allusion to Nehemiah 5:13. Nehemiah commands the people of Judah to no longer oppress the poor among them. He then shakes out the fold of his garment and proclaims, "So may God shake out every man from his house and from his labor who does not keep this promise." This garment or robe would most likely have gathered dust, leaves, and debris which would then fall to the ground. This act symbolized judgment for those who had broken Nehemiah's command. Paul imitates Nehemiah and likewise condemns the Jews by saying that, in effect, God has shaken them out.

But the second part of Paul's response is verbal. He says, "Your blood be on your own heads! I am innocent. From now on I will go to the Gentiles" (Acts **18:6**). This too has its roots in the Old Testament. Ezekiel 33:1-5 describes a watchman's job. A watchman was to survey the land and communicate what he saw to the people. If he saw an enemy coming, he was to blow the trumpet and warn the people. But if the people heard the trumpet and ignored the warning, their blood was on their own heads. The watchman had performed his duty and was now considered innocent if the citizens were to die.

Paul indicates that he is a watchman and has proclaimed a warning of impending danger: spiritual separation from God. But the Jews have heard the trumpet call of the gospel and chosen to reject it. Thus, Paul has done exactly what he was called to do. The people's rejection, resistance, and blasphemy are now their own responsibility. Paul then adds that he is no longer going to spend his time in the synagogue in Corinth, but in Gentile places.

We preach with confidence, knowing we cannot fail. We only fail if we remain silent.

God calls his people to faithfulness, not necessarily fruitfulness. We could not save ourselves. We cannot, therefore, save another person from their sin. Only God can work salvation. Our job, our calling, our mission is to preach the gospel of

Jesus Christ. We do this unapologetically and boldly, and offer the gospel to all people. That is our task and our responsibility. The work of salvation, however, belongs in the sovereign hands of our God. We can, therefore, preach with confidence, knowing that we cannot fail. We only fail if we remain silent.

Paul leaves the Jewish crowd but does not go far. He visits Titius Justus, who lives adjacent to the synagogue (Acts **18:7**). Here Paul worships with other believers. By doing this, Paul continues to demonstrate judgment against the Jews. One of the believers that worshiped with Paul was Crispus (**v 8**). This is an important name, for we read that Crispus was the ruler of the synagogue. Crispus, a Jewish official, was converted through Paul's preaching. Though many Jews rejected Paul, there were some who believed and were baptized. This is similar to what happened in Athens (17:32-34).

Do Not Be Silent

In **18:9-11**, Luke gives some historical background to Paul's extended time in Corinth. In **verse 9**, Luke mentions that the Lord appeared to Paul and encouraged him to press on. Apparently, Paul was in need of comfort after the Jewish rejection. Paul, no doubt, wondered if his presence in Corinth would accomplish any good. The Lord commanded Paul to "not be afraid." He then gave the foundation for that command: "... for I am with you, and no one will attack you to harm you, for I have many in this city who are my people" (**v 9-10**). God enjoined Paul to press on in the gospel work and encouraged him with the news that many in the city would repent. God had his people in the city and Paul would see them come to faith in Christ. God, therefore, commanded Paul to dispense with his fear. Paul had to trust in God's power, provision, and sovereign will. Paul heard this word and believed it. He stayed in Corinth preaching and teaching the word of God there for one year and six months (**v 11**).

The three imperatives given in these verses bear significance for all believers. First, fear must not mark the children of God. Indeed, Paul wrote in Romans 8:15, "For you did not receive the spirit of slavery to fall back into fear." Fear has no place in the household of faith for fear is the very opposite of faith. Second, God's people must always speak and proclaim the gospel. Sharing the faith is not contingent upon our circumstances or trials. Our feelings are not to dictate when we proclaim God's truth. We must go on speaking the good news of the gospel because of the mission God has called his people into. Finally, God says, "Do not be silent." We cannot be silent. The mission is too grave, the consequences too great, the rewards too glorious to remain silent! Eternal souls hang in the balance. We cannot and must not be a silent people for the message we proclaim is nothing less than eternal **redemption**.

God Keeps His Promise

No matter where Paul did ministry, he met opposition. Spiritual advancement will almost always meet satanic opposition. The Jews accused Paul, before the proconsul Gallio, of teaching others to worship a god not allowed under Roman law (Acts **18:12-13**). There was a Roman law prohibiting any individual from converting Roman citizens to a foreign cult or religious faction. With this law in mind, the Jews brought Paul to court, hoping to have him condemned and executed. Even before Paul could defend his case, Gallio declared Paul innocent of the accusation (**v 14**). Gallio dismissed the case because he felt the matter concerned Jewish doctrines and interpretations of their own law (**v 15-16**). The providential hand of God hides in the background of this development in the story. Gallio could have condemned Paul. God, however, worked in the situation and protected Paul from further persecution.

What happens next, in **verse 17**, is not entirely clear. Who seized Sosthenes? Why did they beat him? On these matters, the text is difficult to interpret. Some interpret the "who" as a Gentile mob angry at the Jews for trying to stir up trouble. Other commentators believe Jews are the "who." Those who believe it was the Jews doing the beating differ on the "why." Some believe the Jews held Sosthenes in contempt for his failure to procure a conviction of Paul. Others believe Sosthenes was a Christian, since Paul mentions a Sosthenes as a brother in his introduction to 1 Corinthians. It may be, therefore, that the Jews took their anger out on Sosthenes, whom they suspected to be a Christian. The first option is more likely and fits with the overall flow of the narrative. God's judgment comes upon the Jews for their rejection of the Gospel. As the Jewish leaders try and halt Paul's mission (which is ultimately God's mission), God turns the tables on their efforts and permits swift retribution against the Jewish leader.

Despite the many violent threats and judicial proceedings, the Lord continued to vindicate Paul. The Lord had called him to Corinth and would hold him fast there until it was time to move on. Paul had no reason to fear, for the Lord was with him. Indeed, God has sovereignly placed all his children, in every age, right where he wants them to be.

> God has sovereignly placed all his children, in every age, right where he wants them to be.

fear, for the Lord was with him. Indeed, God has sovereignly placed all his children, in every age, right where he wants them to be. Circumstances never surprise God. Trials, persecution, and difficulty never catch God out. The Scriptures reveal God's intimate knowledge of his people, even to knowing the number of hairs on each head (Luke 12:7). Therefore, fear must never mark a child of God. Fear is incompatible with faith. Fear assumes that God is distant, unacquainted with the trials of his church. This is not the God of the Bible. He knows what his people face, and he will always be with them.

Questions for reflection

1. Paul was a tentmaker and a preacher. How is God calling you to work hard and to be involved in ministry? Are you prioritizing the first over the second in an unhelpful way?

2. What are you afraid of? How does that fear tend to obscure the reality of God's sovereignty and goodness in your life?

3. How does the Lord's encouragement to Paul in verses 9 and 10 comfort you today?

PART TWO

A Peculiar Devotion

Corinth would continue to serve as Paul's city of residence for some time (Acts **18:18**). Paul's continued presence must have meant the tumult chronicled in the previous verses had died down, leaving him in relative freedom to do the work of ministry. Paul often met opposition throughout his missionary journeys. Indeed, fidelity to the gospel provokes hostility from the world. God, however, intends such trials to drive us toward his grace and mercy. The absence of suffering might lead Christians toward complacency or pride. At the same time, Christians should not wish for suffering. When, however, trials do come, God often uses them to decrease our dependence on our own strength, and increase our reliance upon his power.

Despite the sufferings Paul faced, Jesus Christ constantly preserved him, protected him, and bore tremendous fruit through Paul's faithfulness. Even in Corinth, as Paul was on trial for his life, God preserved the gospel witness and providentially orchestrated circumstances in the city to allow Paul's continued presence there. God fostered an environment conducive to the spread of the gospel and the growth of the young Christians in the city. Luke's narrative often calls Christians to observe the faithful providence of God. His word will never return empty or void. He will accomplish his purposes. No power of hell or scheme of man can halt the progress of the gospel throughout the world.

Having stayed in Corinth for some time, Paul begins a journey back to Antioch, probably to report on his progress (**v 18**). Luke notes the presence of Priscilla and Aquila, who accompany Paul all the way to Ephesus. This husband and wife most likely financed Paul's trip. Then, Luke records something peculiar; without any explanation, Luke writes, "At Cenchreae he had cut his hair, for he was under a vow."

The words "hair" and "vow" lead us to the conclusion that Paul had taken the Nazirite vow. Numbers 6:1-21 detail the requirements of the Nazirite vow. The person under the oath would have to abstain from alcohol and the cutting of their hair. At the conclusion of the vow, the individual would cut their hair and have it placed upon the temple altar to be burned as a peace offering. Paul, therefore, cut his hair because he had concluded his vow, and would have kept it in order to burn it at the temple in Jerusalem.

This account probably strikes our modern Gentile minds as bizarre. Indeed, the act seems out of place for the apostle Paul, the apostle to the Gentiles. Why would Paul, who had time and again preached of God's grace and salvation apart from works of the law, engage in an Old Testament ritual? Paul, as a Jew, had the freedom to continue to obey the law. Freed also by the gospel, however, he could engage in the ritual with an entirely new perspective. He may have undertaken in the vow as an act of devotion to God and an expression of thanksgiving. He also may have entered into it in order to appease the Christian leaders in Jerusalem, who still held their Jewish heritage in high regard and esteem.

Christians should learn from Paul's example. The law did not bind Paul to a Nazirite vow. Even under the old covenant, the Nazirite vow was voluntary. Paul entered into the vow, most likely, as an act of love for his Jewish brothers in the faith who were still squeamish about the inclusion of Gentiles in the family of God. Paul does not chide Jewish Christians. Instead, he deals with them tenderly, and even engages in a vow that he is under no obligation to take. 1 Corinthians 9:19-20 says:

"For though I am free from all, I have made myself a servant to all, that I might win more of them. To the Jews I became as a Jew, in order to win Jews. To those under the law I became as one under the law (though not being myself under the law) that I might win those under the law."

Paul willingly surrendered his rights for the spiritual advancement of others. He devoted his life to enriching the lives of others. He laid down his freedoms out love for those whom God had called him to serve. Christians have much to learn from Paul's example. So often, Christians fail to love others because they have calculated the sacrifice as too costly. Christian love, however, counts no cost. Indeed, as Paul says in Philippians 2:3, "Do nothing from selfish ambition or conceit, but in humility count others more significant than yourselves."

A Singular Devotion

In Ephesus, Paul preached in the synagogues as he often had done throughout his journeys (Acts **18:19**). His time with the Jews seems to have gone well because they asked Paul to stay for a longer period of time (**v 20**). Paul, however, declined.

Paul's rebuff may seem rude or unwarranted. After all, when people respond to the message of the gospel, is it not right to stay and continue the work of ministry? The answer to that question, however, as Paul shows us, does not depend on our feelings or expectations. Staying or going, silence or speaking, all depends upon the will of God. Paul devoted himself exclusively to the will of the Father. He says in **verse 21** that he would return if God willed. Paul was willing to leave because God willed him to leave. However, Paul also indicated his desire to return, so long as that fit within God's preordained plan.

Again, the minor details of Luke's narrative pack a powerful applications for modern-day Christians. Paul centered his vision on the will of God. In success or failure, conversions or condemnation, salvation or stoning, Paul remained committed to God's will—even if that meant leaving a place or people in a time of ministry fruitfulness. Paul's actions, however, do raise the question, "How do we know the will of God, especially in the absence of a clear Scriptural command?" The answer to this question involves many nuances and difficulties depending on the circumstances. Generally, however, Christians must base their decision on the Scriptures. The word of God abounds with wisdom and lessons for life. Furthermore, God has made clear what his will is for our lives in several texts. As Paul says in 1 Thessalonians 4:3, "For this is the will of God, your **sanctification**…" Our growth in

Christ-likeness remains God's single vision and will for our life. When you approach a difficult decision and wonder what God's will might be, press in on the Scriptures, pray ardently for God's direction, and trust that in whatever decision you make, God will be with you.

Acts **18:22-23** details Paul's return to Antioch. He spends time there, no doubt encouraging the church with news from his missionary journeys. After his time in Antioch, Paul makes his way north into Galatia and Phrygia, encouraging the disciples and churches which he and his companions have planted.

A Humble Devotion

Luke's narrative takes a break from the ministry of Paul and shifts to Apollos. Apollos hailed from Alexandria, a prominent ancient city (**v 24**). Alexandria boasted a huge Jewish population, and Apollos himself was a Jew. It was in Alexandria that the Old Testament was translated into Greek. (This translation is known as the Septuagint.) Apollos's eloquence and education in the Scriptures probably stem from his Alexandrian origins.

Apollos had been instructed in the way of the Lord (**v 25**). Geographically, Alexandria was in north Egypt, some distance from the apostolic happenings in Palestine. This verse, however, indicates Apollos's knowledge of "the baptism of John." Therefore, he must have traveled to the Judean region and been introduced to John the Baptist's teaching. His upbringing in the Scriptures and his encounter with teachings of John the Baptist enabled Apollos to speak with fervor and accuracy (**v 25-26**). He preached boldly the things concerning Jesus.

Despite his bold, fervent, and accurate teaching, something remained deficient in Apollos's instruction. Indeed, his knowledge only extended to the teachings of John the Baptist. John's teaching was incomplete because it only predicted and anticipated the ministry of the Messiah. In 19:1-7, Luke recounts Paul's encounter with other Christians who only knew the baptism of John. These disciples did not even know there was a Holy Spirit. Apollos, however, does not seem to have been so deficient in his knowledge. Luke records in **18:26**, "He began to speak boldly in the synagogue, but when Priscilla and Aquila heard him, they took him aside and explained to him the way of God more accurately."

Set yourself within the context of the narrative and in the shoes of Apollos. You are a highly educated Jew, trained in the Scriptures in one of the most prominent cities in the ancient world. You have come to a saving faith in Jesus Christ and have been trained as his disciple. You come to Ephesus and use your skills of eloquence and knowledge of the Scriptures to speak powerfully about the things of Christ. Then, after you have preached out your heart to your brothers and sisters in the faith, a man and his wife pull you aside and correct your teaching. How would you have responded?

> Set yourself in the shoes of Apollos. How would you have responded?

Apollos responded with humility and received correction from his brother and sister in Christ. In this instance, Aquila and Priscilla recognized Apollos as a gifted and powerful teacher, who needed help on some issues. Apollos, with profound maturity, received their instructions with humility. He could have rebuffed them because of his status. He could have refuted their instruction by leaning on his educational background. Through an outrageous display of pride, he could have rejected help and pressed on in an ungodly, rugged individualism.

On the other hand, Priscilla and Aquila exuded a godly maturity in stepping in to correct their brother. When they recognized a deficiency, they stepped in to help. Their actions not only served Apollos but also those who could benefit from Apollos' gifted teaching. The actions of Aquila and Priscilla should remind Christians of the joy and grace of fellowship in the body of Christ. God has gifted his people with a multiplicity of talents designed to serve the church. Priscilla and Aquila used the gifts God had given them to correct their brother and ensure that his teaching exuded greater faithfulness and doctrinal fidelity.

Apollos's response challenges the pride which resides deep within the recesses of our hearts. None of us like to be told we were wrong or came up short. In such moments, Satan tempts us to harden our hearts and shift the blame onto others. Indeed, Satan wants nothing less than to disrupt the fellowship of the church and to render the gifts of God's people ineffective. Had Priscilla and Aquila remained silent, they would have given in to the temptation to prioritize their self-preservation—another form of pride—for fear of a harsh response from Apollos. Had Apollos responded with resentment or anger, he too would have been guilty of pride.

Pride destroys the community of Christ, whether through silence when we need to speak or through our response when a brother or sister confronts us with our sin. This episode in Acts 18 shows the beauty of God's gifts to his people and the joy of Christian love. When God's people dispel pride, they strengthen the bond between God's people and enable a more fruitful and effective ministry for the church.

Indeed, in the next two verses, we see the fruit of humble devotion to God. Luke records that when Apollos arrived in Achaia, his preaching had an even greater effect, and it strengthened the church exponentially (**v 27**). Moreover, Luke writes, "For he powerfully refuted the Jews in public, showing by the Scriptures that the Christ was Jesus" (**v 28**). The humility of Priscilla and Aquila in dispensing with fear and correcting their brother, and Apollos's humble response, enable a more powerful preaching ministry which extolled the glories of Christ. When God's people exude a humble devotion, the body of Christ grows in strength and, most importantly, in love.

Christians today need a healthy dose of the humble devotion displayed in this narrative account. Pride is a dangerous sin and an old enemy going back to the fall in Genesis 3. Pride kills fellowship. God's people, therefore, must embrace humility as a hallmark of their devotion. When a brother or sister confronts you because of sin, do not resist. Rather, receive their rebuke with humility and search your heart for any grievous way within. Thank your fellow believer for the correction and their courage in taking such an action. Furthermore, do not let pride keep you silent. Humility will lead you to correct your brothers and sisters in kindness and in grace. Indeed, a humble heart will have as an aim the growth in maturity of your fellow believers and of the church in its Christ-likeness.

Questions for reflection

1. Again, we see Paul surrendering his rights for the cause of the gospel. Since this was first noted in this book, how have you had opportunity to do the same in your life—and did you take that opportunity?

2. What does Apollos' response to correction teach you about receiving rebukes? Why is it a good thing to have people around you who are willing to correct you?

3. Is there anyone for whom you could serve as a Priscilla or an Aquila? How? What would hold you back from doing that?

6. REPENTANCE AND RIOTS

In Acts 19, we find Paul in Ephesus, a place where he's been before (18:19-21). While there, Paul used his brief time to train, build, mentor, disciple, and send out a core of pastors, leaders, and preachers. Thus, Ephesus became a hub of church-planting activity and held a special place in Paul's heart.

Disciples—But of Whom?

When Paul arrived at Ephesus the second time, he found local disciples (**19:1**). Their designation as "disciples" is crucial. The designation raises the question, disciples of what? Who or what did these "disciples" believe in? It appears they held to an "almost Christianity." They believed as much as they had been taught to believe. They did not, however, know about the Holy Spirit (**v 2**). Paul, therefore, saw it necessary to question them further and to teach them, affirming the significance of baptism in the life of a believer (**v 3**). These disciples claimed to possess a true baptism yet had not even heard of the Holy Spirit. Similarly, Christians today must exercise caution and wisdom when dealing with someone who claims to follow Christ but fails to exhibit the fruit of the Spirit. Just because someone claims to follow Jesus does not mean that they have truly been saved. We should ask, does this person actually profess the gospel? And how does this person's life evidence the transformative power of the gospel?

The disciples inform Paul that they were baptized into John the Baptist's baptism. Paul recognizes a prime evangelistic moment and utilizes his conversation with these disciples to share the gospel (**v 4**). In doing so, Paul models how to move people from what we might call an incipient faith—that is, an anticipatory faith—into the fullness of the Christian faith. Notice how directly Paul does it. He says that if they were baptized into John's baptism, they ought to at least follow John's teaching. But if they really understood John's baptism, they would understand that John himself preached the salvation that comes through Jesus Christ. In other words, the baptism that John practiced pointed to the baptism of Jesus Christ. Their baptism anticipated the better baptism that has now come. The fulfillment of the disciples' baptism could only come through the baptism of faith in Jesus Christ. Paul's message proves effective as they come to confess Jesus as Lord (**v 5**).

When the apostle laid his hands on them, the Holy Spirit indwelled them, which caused all twelve in the group to speak in tongues and **prophesy** (**v 6-7**). This outward sign confirmed the inward spiritual reality that had taken place in their hearts. Four occasions like this occur in the book of Acts, but we should not view this kind of sign as normative for the Christian church across all the ages. The event described here occurs in the context of apostolic ministry. The church today does not operate within this same context. Believers today, however, must recognize how Paul educated these confused disciples. Paul lovingly corrects these disciples and boldly points to the deficiencies present in their faith. We ought to demonstrate the same wisdom, grace, and confidence in the gospel message when we have opportunities to correct our confused contemporaries. At the same time, beware always trying to "be right." Pride can lead a person to a nitpicky judgmentalism that fails to exude compassion and gentleness when dealing with others.

> Beware always trying to "be right." Pride can lead to a nitpicky jugdmentalism.

Persistent Preaching and Real Growth

In **verse 8**, Paul returns to his basic missiological methodology; he first finds out if there are any disciples in a city, and then goes to the synagogue to preach. Like his Lord, Paul spent much of his time teaching where he knew Jews would gather. He was the apostle to the Gentiles, but that did not negate the reality that the gospel is "to the Jew first" (Romans 1:16).

While he preached in the synagogue, Paul would reason with the Jews according to the Scripture and would plead with them to confess that the Messiah had come in Jesus Christ. Paul's message, therefore, echoes Jesus' own message—the Messiah has come, and so too has the kingdom of God. The coming of Christ has inaugurated the long-expected kingdom of God. This kingdom, however, did not come through a brilliant military conquest of worldly rulers. Christ established his rule over the cosmos through his humble death on the cross. Through his life, death, resurrection, and ascension, Christ ushered in the beginnings of the kingdom, which will culminate in resplendent power upon the second coming of the King.

Paul was met with two responses to this. Some embraced and believed the message, but others rejected Christ, even going so far as to slander Christ's followers (Acts **19:9**). Such a response should not surprise us. To reject the gospel message is to reject the one who preaches the gospel message. That is what happened to Paul and his disciples in the synagogue. When the people of God proclaim the gospel in faithfulness, they will meet open and eager hostility. Christians must not, however, lose heart upon rejection. God reigns supreme over the cosmos and providentially governs all things according to the good and perfect purposes of his will. Rejection, therefore, cannot paralyze the faithful disciple who, with assurance in God's goodness, boldly advances the message of the gospel. At the same time, when someone rejects the gospel, they ultimately reject God. Christians therefore, summon all to repent and believe, knowing that all will be held to account for their response to the gospel of Jesus Christ.

In response to rejection, Paul and the disciples withdrew and began looking for another place into which to take the hope of the gospel. Luke tells us that they went to the hall of Tyrannus, a school of **rhetoric**, where they spent two years preaching the word of God and making new disciples. Thus, **verse 10**, like the whole book of Acts, helps us understand how early Christianity spread out of the synagogue and into the rest of the world—to the Jew first and then to the Greek also. It also helps us understand the means through which the message of Christianity spread—through the faithful, persistent preaching of God's word.

Invoking a Name You Don't Know

In the next section, Luke continues to show us that God accomplished glorious things through the power of Paul's ministry. "Extraordinary" is a word rightly translated (**v 11**). Evil spirits succumbed to the power of God and fled before the preaching of his word. God even healed people as they merely touched Paul's garments (**v 12**). Nothing ordinary rises from this scene. Luke carefully points to the power of God as the impetus for the powerful workings which he demonstrated through his willing servant Paul.

Notice, too, the reference to evil spirits here. We must be careful in our day not to become too "sophisticated" to believe in the existence of evil spirits. When we do, we become too "sophisticated" for the worldview of the early church, of Paul and the apostles—and of Jesus Christ. Even the Jews had an understanding of demons, as evidenced by the role of itinerant Jewish exorcists (**v 13**).

The Jews in the ancient world had a particular reputation for being able to cast out demons. In first-century Asia Minor, exorcism could be a lucrative business venture. Those with the franchise on the practice were the Jews, which only further testified to the power of God's word, particularly that of the **Torah**. The seven sons of Sceva evidently wanted to get in on the business (**v 14**), and did so by trying to invoke the name of Jesus. They recognized Paul had power, but they did not know the One by whom he had power, so they tried to invoke Jesus by name-checking Paul. Their actions demonstrate the foolishness in attempting to leverage the name of Christ for commercial motives rather than humbly submitting to the saving power of the gospel.

Like the sons of Sceva, many in our own day similarly call upon Jesus without really knowing him. All around us are people ready to call upon the Lord Jesus but do not want the gospel. They are ready to call upon a sweet Jesus who will be their constant companion and spiritual talisman, but they are not interested in knowing Jesus as the incarnate Son of God. They want a Jesus they can use, not a Jesus who saves. The "prosperity gospel" movement invokes the name of Christ, prays in the name of God, and claims his promise and blessing all for financial security rather than eternal salvation. Other times, however, genuine Christians permit this kind of attitude in their own heart. They can, if they lose sight of the biblical expectations of Christian living, think that because they follow Jesus, life will exude peace and comfort. Christians can adopt a sense of entitlement which demands a certain way of life from Jesus. This, however, is not biblical discipleship. To follow Christ means denying ourselves, including our culturally-shaped expectations of this life, and taking up our cross.

The Word Prevails

In **verse 15**, an evil spirit answers the sons of Sceva. We ought not pass over these words too quickly. The demon claim to "know" Jesus. James 2:19 reminds us that demons know things about God, but they do not know him in the way that saves. The demon intellectually assents to the knowledge of Jesus, but does not trust him as a sufficient Savior for sins. The demon is proof that intellectual assent to Jesus, as necessary as it is for salvation, is not enough for salvation.

"But who are you?" is one of the most pathetic and humiliating questions asked in all of Scripture (Acts **19:15**). The evil spirit knows who Jesus is and recognizes the power that Paul exercises, but knows nothing of the sons of Sceva. The only thing the evil spirit recognizes about them is that they are imposters who have no business giving him orders by invoking the name of Christ.

As if being dressed down by an evil spirit isn't humiliating enough, the sons of Sceva are also physically attacked by the possessed man in **verse 16**. Imagine the sheer terror of having a demon strip you naked of all your pretensions and demonstrate the falsity of your message and entire ministry. And then imagine being one of those who witnessed such an incredible scene. No wonder this became known through Ephesus (**v 17**). For a Jewish man, and still more for seven sons of a high priest, being naked before others was far worse than being wounded. To be naked was to be exposed in your emptiness, idolatry, and impotence of faith. To be stripped naked was to be shamed and humiliated in the highest form.

This reminds us that the Lord has his way of making sure that the name of Jesus Christ is praised, even if it comes at the expense of seven sons of a high priest. We saw earlier in the chapter how the word of the Lord prevailed even though Paul was kicked out of the synagogue. Though the Jews try to prevent the gospel message from spreading, the Lord continues to work so that the name of Jesus is known throughout Asia Minor, among both Jews and Greeks.

The results of this extraordinary encounter with the power of God was remarkable. The Holy Spirit convicted many believers of their idolatry and **syncretism**—mixing magical arts with devotion to Christ. They came confessing and bringing their paraphernalia of witchcraft and divination to be burned (**v 18-19**). The value of what they burned—fifty thousand pieces of silver's worth of idolatrous articles—testified to the power of the gospel and the preached word of God. The idolatry of Ephesus ended up in an ash heap, while the word of the Lord continued to increase and prevail mightily (**v 20**). Here in Ephesus, Luke provides a demonstration of the nature of true repentance. It is a repentance that is both costly and public. Turning to Christ necessitates a decisive repudiation of the rule of all others in order to come under the unmatched and supreme lordship of Jesus Christ.

Such a powerful passage reminds us that our job as believers is not to try to become known to the demons as exorcists or because of our extraordinary powers. Our task is to make sure we are known in hell because of our faithful and bold preaching of God's word. If we are faithful in keeping ourselves anchored in God's word, we will never run the risk of having an evil spirit confront us and say, "Jesus, I know, and Paul I recognize, but who are you?" By God's grace, the evil spirits will know us by name.

Questions for reflection

1. How does Paul's model of engaging with the disciples he discovers in Ephesus shape your own approach to speaking with those you know who are theologically confused?

2. Is there any way in which you're in danger of wanting a Jesus you can use, rather than a Jesus who will save?

3. What do the Ephesian converts show us about repentance? Is this what repentance looks like in your life?

PART TWO

After watching the word of the Lord prevail mightily in Ephesus, Paul felt it right to go to Jerusalem in time for the **Passover**, and then on to Rome (**v 21**). As the apostle to the Gentiles, Paul recognized the need to go to Rome, the center of the Gentile universe.

On his way, though, he was going to send out Timothy, Erastus, and Titus (who is not mentioned here in Acts) into Macedonia to spread the gospel (**v 22**). In Romans 16:23, we read that Erastus was the city treasurer. He was a man of great means and tremendous importance. He would have had enormous freedom to travel. This proved to be a valuable asset to the early church, and it shows how God sovereignly uses people and their circumstances for the sake of is kingdom.

The Great Disturbance

Acts **19:23** is one of the most understated verses in all the Bible. Just when things were supposed to go according to Paul's plans, a seismic disturbance shook things up. "The Way" was shorthand for the Christian Church and its gospel, and a man named Demetrius was greatly perturbed by its progress and its potential to disturb his way of life (**v 24**). Demetrius was a silversmith. Silver was plentiful in this region and fueled the Gentile economy, as it was heavily used in art and idol-making. Demetrius made shrines to Artemis, also known as Aphrodite, the goddess of love.

Artemis' temple was located in Ephesus. It was one of the "Seven Wonders of the Ancient World" as it was the biggest building in existence at the time. Made of marble, the structure stood approximately 425 feet (130m) long, 220 feet (67m) wide, and 60 feet (18m) tall, supported by 127 marble columns. It was engineered by precisely cut marble blocks that perfectly fit together. No city was as proud of its glorious structures as Ephesus was of this temple. Without the temple, the city would have lost its claim to cultural pre-eminence. Demetrius' business capitalized on this. Yet, with the spread of Paul's gospel, which was unashamedly subversive of the pagan economy, the silversmith was losing business. So, in an effort to save his business, he felt it necessary to rise up and make a public push against Christianity (**v 25**). It is evident, therefore, that the gospel invades every sphere of life. Even economic policies cannot escape from the transformative power of the gospel. When the gospel comes into contact with other ways of "doing life," it will cause friction. The gospel confronts the sinfulness inherent in the systems of our society. When Christians proclaim the gospel, they will not only meet lost souls but will expose immoral institutions that war

> The gospel invades every sphere: even economic policies cannot escape from the transformative power of the gospel.

against the principles of the **biblical ethic**. In a post-Christian world, therefore, there will sometimes be no way for the gospel and society to peacefully co-exist, and the backlash from the society might be fierce, particularly when the gospel threatens livelihoods.

Demetrius' major charge against Paul was that he claimed that gods made with human hands were not gods at all (**v 26**). Paul, as a good Jew, knew the **Shema** (Deuteronomy 6:4). He understood that God is one, so he proclaimed that any other god is necessarily no god at all. Paul did not stand alone in this monotheistic belief. Consider Elijah's boldness at Mount Carmel in 1 Kings 18:22-39 or Isaiah's words in Isaiah 40:18-20 and 44:9-17. It does not take a second glance to see their stark condemnation of idols. The default position of the ancient mind, however, was pagan idolatry, and a certain amount of respect was expected for every local deity. Paul was not afraid of these idols and the pagan worldview; he confronted them head on.

Modern Westerners are just as idolatrous. We often worship ideas, ambition, or power as objects of idolatry. In the same ludicrous way, we take something less than God and render to it worship, of which only God is worthy. Similarly, Christians run the risk of functionally adopting a syncretistic worldview wherein we look the other way when people worship another god. This syncretism can also allow secular worldviews like the American Dream to contaminate the purity of the gospel and Christian discipleship, and pervert true Christian living. Paul's condemnation of this syncretism and idolatry meant disaster for Demetrius' business. If Artemis was no deity at all, no one would spend their money on her shrines. The stupidity of idolatry presents itself in this narrative. If indeed Artemis reigned as a powerful and magnificent goddess, would she really need the work of a mere silversmith to defend her honor?! But the idol- and shrine-makers understood that if Paul persuaded others, they would be out of business and Artemis would be forsaken (Acts **19:27**). Christianity was not just an attack upon the **occult** alone but upon paganism of every form. Something had to be done to stop Paul.

In response to Demetrius' speech, the people chant, "Great is Artemis." Demetrius then provokes a riot (**v 28-30**). Hysteria breaks out in the city and the people, enraged and confused, begin grabbing any Christians within reach and dragging them into the large public theater. Paul wanted to go to defend himself, his friends, and his gospel, but the believers kept him from doing so for fear that he would be torn limb from limb. Even the Asiarchs—probably Jewish leaders dispersed throughout Asia—did not want him to go (**v 31**). Though this mob had murder and mayhem in mind, Paul thought that preaching the gospel was worth putting himself in harm's way for. He saw the need to go, but was held back.

A Counter-Cultural Message

At the heart of this riot was the monotheism of the Christian faith, but many in the crowd did not even know this (**v 32**). They were just angry to be angry. Monotheism is the defining theological issue in the context of religious pluralism. In first-century pagan culture, religious pluralism was rampant. Rome believed it was in its own best interests to maintain a hierarchy of gods, incorporating local deities into that structure rather than deny their existence. They argued that their gods were superior to the other gods. This explains why Paul had the licence to preach freely. The Roman Empire did not consider itself greatly threatened by these other religious claims, so long as they were presented in an orderly fashion, were not subversive of Rome, and did not lead to any kind of public disturbance.

Such is not the case in the twenty-first century. Richard Dawkins, one of today's most extreme **militant atheists**, and author of the books *The Selfish Gene* and *The God Delusion,* believes not only that God doesn't exist but also that the very idea of God is dangerous. He argues that belief in God leads people to do dangerous things. According to Dawkins, the most dangerous form of religion is any that believes that their god is the only god. This isn't a unique position. Wendy Kaminer, a very popular columnist, argues that monotheism leads to **exclusivist** thinking, religious wars, and violence.

Upholding monotheistic belief in the face of secular culture is no easy task for the Christian. As in Ephesus, the masses will attempt to drown out our message with their own (**v 33-34**). However, Christians need not shrink back in fear at this kind of opposition. Indeed, Christians must discern the difference between those who start the riots and those who merely shout a pagan mantra because that seems to be the popular anthem. Believers should not let intimidation grip their hearts when they encounter a person very confident in their own position on, for instance, the incompatibility of religion and science or the authority of the Scriptures. Behind the confident tone may be nothing more than a foundation built on sand. Good questions will reveal the shakiness of a person's worldview and will challenge them to think over their views. Indeed, Christians can have the "audacity", based upon the truth of God's word, to say there is only one God and that he has revealed himself in Jesus Christ, his Son. Such a claim is not just politically incorrect but offensive and irrational to the secular mind. This is the kind of claim, however, that Christians must make. It is the same kind of claim Paul and the early believers made in Ephesus.

Innocence and Intervention

As the riot in Ephesus continues, the town clerk shows up. He was a man of enormous responsibility. The town clerk represented the civic authority; he was a local official that served as the chief operating officer of Ephesus. He came to restore order and peace. Rome hated riots. They disrupted the political and societal status quo and fostered an environment of rebellion. The clerk took a brilliant approach to the problem. He started out by simply reassuring the people of Ephesus with what they already knew—that Artemis and her city were great (**v 35**). Since everyone knew this, he contended that there was no reason to riot (**v 36**). He acknowledged that a few held a different position, but there was a right way and a wrong way to deal with it. The wrong way was rioting. But the right way was lawfully through court, which he essentially said was now in session (**v 38**). He implied that if this matter was not dealt with lawfully, then charges would be brought against the rioters (**v 39-40**). In other words, he says, "If you have charges to bring against these men, bring them, but if you do not disperse this riot, charges will be brought against you."

But pay careful attention to **verse 37**. The town clerk outlines a two-part charge of which he declares the Christians innocent. The first, of being "sacrilegious," likely implied a charge of robbing the temple. Temple-robbing was a really big business. Pagan temples fascinated robbers for several reasons. First, pagan temples were architectural gems. People could crack off a corner of the temple of Artemis and sell it for a large profit. Second, the idols themselves were coated with precious stones and metals. The gifts brought to the idols, however, enticed the robbers above anything else. The idol was like a big Christmas tree with nice—and expensive—gifts all around it. Gaius, Aristarchus, and the other believers in Ephesus, however, had no interest in stealing from the temple; the town clerk recognized that Christians would not do this.

The clerk's next point is even more interesting. He denied that these men were "blasphemers of our goddess." Either the clerk did not understand what was going on, or he did understand and decided he could not allow this kind of riot to become a punitive trial. In other words, he had a judgment call to make, and recognized that the thing to be more worried about was the riot, not the blasphemy of his goddess. Whatever the case, the clerk merely wanted to bring order to the situation and defuse the conflict in order to give a good report to Caesar. And just like that, the crowd was dismissed and the chapter ends (**v 41**).

We see in the conclusion, then, that the Christians lived, by the grace of God, to see another day. God sovereignly used the pagan town clerk to spare the lives and bold witness of these believers. Other times, however, riots would take place and Christians would fall to the martyr's sword. Even so, Christians can take comfort in the surpassing sovereignty of our God. In each circumstance, God works all things together according to the purposes of his will. What some intend for evil, God leverages for eternal good. Even the pagan rulers bow to the omnipotent hand of our God. Believers, therefore, must take heart in all circumstances and rest in the perfect, **providential** care of our Father in heaven.

Questions for reflection

1. How do you see "the Way" creating a disturbance in today's society?

2. Paul confronted the idolatry he faced in Ephesus head-on. What issue, either personal or cultural, might God be calling you to specifically confront head-on?

3. Are you honestly willing to court unpopularity in order to serve and speak of the gospel?

7. FAREWELL TO THE ELDERS

Throughout the book of Acts, Luke provides chronological details about Paul's missionary journeys. The beginning of Acts 20 is one example: "After the uproar ceased, Paul sent for the disciples, and after encouraging them, he said farewell and departed for Macedonia" (**v 1**). Luke records real history as it unfolds. He records the sovereign plan and providence of God in the expansion of the gospel through the apostle Paul.

Ephesus is in Asia Minor, which is modern-day Turkey. Luke notes that Paul traveled "through those regions" (**20:2**), meaning that Paul traveled by land from Ephesus through Macedonia to get to Greece. Paul could have simply taken a ship across the Aegean Sea, but instead, he chose to travel by land so that he could visit the believers along the way. Paul utilized his travels to encourage the churches throughout the Roman Empire.

God's Plan Unfolds

Chronology is important in the book of Acts because it demonstrates God's sovereign plan for the world as it unfolds through the lives of the apostles. Paul likely left Ephesus in May of AD 55. That date is assumed because Paul mentioned his intention to leave Ephesus after **Pentecost** in his first letter to the Corinthian believers (1 Corinthians 16:8). The events of Acts **20:1-3** are also explained in 1 Corinthians 16 and 2 Corinthians 1 – 7. Reading these in tandem, we can see that the following events occurred during the three months between Paul's arrival in Greece and his intended departure toward Syria mentioned in Acts **20:3**:

- He intended to use the stay in Greece to collect money for the Jerusalem Christians (1 Corinthians 16:1-4).

- He completed his collection throughout Macedonia (2 Corinthians 8:1-5).

- He stayed in Corinth or nearby in its port city, Cenchreae, for three months. (1 Corinthians 16:5-6).

- He likely penned his great work of theology, the **Epistle** to the Romans, during this time (Romans 16:1, 23).

Paul hoped to return to Jerusalem for Pentecost. Two Pentecosts so closely mentioned in the text might confuse the reader. Luke reveals that Paul wanted to return to Jerusalem before spring of the following year, AD 56, so that he could present the collection to the struggling church in Jerusalem. Even so, Paul faced opposition from Jewish leaders, forcing him to modify his travel plans. Instead of taking the sea route, Paul decided to return over land through Macedonia (Acts **20:3**).

He was not alone, though, and was accompanied by many emerging leaders in the church. The names and locations listed in **verse 4** demonstrate the incredible spread of the gospel out of Jerusalem and Antioch throughout all Asia Minor, Galatia, and beyond into Macedonia and Greece. Luke also accompanied Paul.

Luke provides us with another chronological marker as they journeyed from Macedonia through Philippi. Those listed in this verse went ahead of Paul and Luke with the intention of reuniting with them in Troas. The smaller party sailed out of Philippi toward Troas before the rest followed on and were reunited with them (**v 5-6**). The mention of seemingly minor details like times and locations may seem tedious to the reader. These destinations and timestamps, however, bolster the historicity of the Scriptures. Luke does the work of a fine historian as he laces his narrative together with the geographic progression of Paul's mission.

A Sunday Miracle

Timestamps also serve another important function in this chapter. **Verse 7** marks the first mention in the New Testament of Christian worship on the first day of the week—on what we call Sunday. Christians shifted their day of worship from the Jewish Sabbath to the Lord's Day to commemorate the resurrection of the Lord Jesus Christ.

This is no ordinary gathering for bread. In Acts, the phrase "breaking bread" always refers to the Lord's Supper with a fellowship meal (see 2:42, 46, and so on). These Christians gathered for worship on the first day of the week. It appears, in this instance, that the gathering was taking place in the evening around dinnertime.

Preachers like to use **20:7** as their justification for long-winded preaching. When the clock strikes midnight, Paul's preaching does not cease. Surprisingly, things get more interesting in the twilight hours of this narrative as Luke sets the scene for a Sunday miracle. Luke writes, "There were many lamps in the upper room where we were gathered. And a young man named Eutychus, sitting at the window, sank into a deep sleep as Paul talked still longer" (**v 8-9**). Lamps in a room did not merely serve to provide light but also warmth. A full belly, a warm room, and a long-winded talk spell potential disaster for a listener whose seat of choice is an open window on the third story of a building. Eutychus falls asleep during Paul's preaching. The consequence? He plummets to his untimely demise.

Luke retells the story to elicit sympathy for Eutychus—a name which, ironically, means "fortunate." Fortune, however, did not rescue Eutychus. The providential and gracious power of God would come to his rescue. Apart from the resurrection of Jesus and of those who were raised from the dead at the moment of his death (Matthew 27:51-53), there are only seven cases in the whole Bible where human beings are raised from the dead. There are two in the Old Testament, both by the power of God's Spirit, when Elijah and Elisha raise individuals from the dead. Jesus himself raises three from the dead to show his own authority over death itself: Jairus' daughter, the young man of Nain, and, famously, Lazarus. Two apostles, by the Spirit's power, also raise the dead to life. The first is Peter, who sees Dorcus return to life. The last is Paul, who raises Eutychus.

Paul knows his Old Testament and remembers how Elijah and Elisha prayed for the life of those young boys to return to them (1 Kings 17:21; 2 Kings 4:32–35), so he does the same. Luke records that Paul bends over Eutychus and takes him in his arms (Acts **20:10**). As God's power was demonstrated through his prophets in the Old Testament, so God's divine power manifests itself in splendor when the young man comes back to life. Paul stays in Troas through until the morning (**v 11**). The church here is willing to stay listening as long as Paul continues talking. They leave, greatly comforted, only after he departs (**v 12**). Luke then describes the beginning of Paul's return to Jerusalem—a return which will shift the narrative of Acts into its long conclusion focusing on Paul's imprisonment (**v 13-15**).

> One day every Christian will experience more than Eutychus did.

This narrative should call us to the power of the gospel and the preaching of the Lord Jesus Christ. Too often, churches manipulate narratives like that of Acts 20 to build a ministry around healing and miracles. Paul, however, focused on the proclamation of the gospel. The word of God stood as the centerpiece of Paul's ministry. This was not a miracle service interrupted by a word of preaching. This was preaching interrupted by a miracle. The true miracle, though, flows from the power of the gospel itself to raise spiritually dead men and women to eternal life. Though no Christian today should expect to experience what Eutychus did, every Christian will experience more than he did. One day, Christ will raise us all up from the grave, and on that day we will be brought into an eternal life.

Christians today need not give up on nor doubt the power of the preached Word. The world feels the pangs of sin and suffers under the grip of Satan. The power of God for salvation, however, resounds through the preaching of his word. The preached word, by God's grace, breaks the chains, lifts the veil, and sets the captive free.

Ministering to the Leaders

The time has come for Paul to say his farewell to the Ephesians. He plans to speak to the elders of the church. He does not, however, speak to them in Ephesus. Instead, he calls them to Miletus, some 50 miles (80 km) from Ephesus (**v 17**). Why would Paul do this? Luke gives us Paul's motivation in **verse 16**: "... so that he might not have to spend time in Asia, for he was hastening to be at Jerusalem, if possible, on the day of Pentecost." Paul's actions might be misinterpreted as lack of interest in the church and a coldness which leads him to summon the leaders of the church to himself.

In fact, Paul, as so often, has a strategic, Christ-centered impulse which drives his mission. Paul has intentionally disengaged himself from the direct oversight and leadership of the Ephesian church. When Paul first moved into a given region, he would go to the synagogue and preach to the Jews. He would then preach to the Gentiles. After he had established a church, he would work to grow the congregation organically through indigenous leadership. His ultimate goal was to have a local, autonomous, self-sufficient congregation. The churches in the region are needy, and he realizes that if he visits with them, he will be unable to make it to Jerusalem by Pentecost. Sometimes, leaders have to make strategic sacrifices in order to accomplish the mission. Paul did not "decide to sail past Ephesus, so that he might not have to spend time in Asia" (**v 16**) out of coldness but rather, because he had another priority.

A leader's time is never wasted in developing other leaders, and Paul has a gospel interest in ensuring that the church at Ephesus has healthy elders. So, "from Miletus he sent to Ephesus and called the elders of the church to come to him" (**v 17**). This is Paul's strategic disengagement from Ephesus—he's not leaving them without leadership. Paul, instead, ensures that his legacy will continue through the faithful leadership of well-equipped and trained elders who will preach the word of God and proclaim the excellencies of Christ to the people of the region. Paul, therefore, models the ideal Christian leader. He knows his limits. He knows his humanity. But he also knows that the work of Christ reigns supreme. He therefore trains his replacements and purposefully stations himself to recede into the shadows. This is truly humble and Christ-centered leadership.

Paul's style, however, contradicts much of what we see in contemporary evangelicalism. Some leaders build the ministry around themselves rather than around the Lord Jesus Christ. This disease spreads to and infects every corner of the ministry as its leader begins to believe that he is indispensable. Indeed, we have seen entire ministries forfeit their identity as children of God in order to set on the throne human authorities and personalities. Paul, however, draws the Ephesians elders to himself and begins a commissioning which places the care of the congregation into their hands. Paul demonstrates to all that the ministry of Christ must be about Christ. No person may share the throne which belongs only to Jesus. Some, by God's grace, will wield incredible influence. This influence, however, derives from God. We live as caretakers, undershepherds, and servants of the God of the universe. Paul understood this and did everything he could to raise up the next generation of men who would faithfully execute the office of elder. Paul built his mission not around his own fame but around the fame and exaltation of Jesus Christ.

Questions for reflection

1. Notice that Paul's priorities were always the strengthening of the churches and the establishing of new ones. Your calling and context will be very different than the apostle's, but how are you living out the same priorities as him?

2. "Though no Christian today should expect to experience what Eutychus did, every Christian will experience more than he did" at that point. What do you make of this view? How does it give you a realistic view of today, and an exciting view of your future?

3. "A leader's time is never wasted in developing other leaders." Are you in a position to develop others? Or could you ask someone more mature in the faith to help you develop your gifts and ministries?

PART TWO

Paul's Legacy

From his farewell speech, we not only see the strategy of Paul but we also see the character of his legacy. He is able to say to the elders:

"You yourselves know how I lived among you the whole time from the first day that I set foot in Asia, serving the Lord with all humility and with tears and with trials that happened to me through the plots of the Jews; how I did not shrink from declaring to you anything that was profitable, and teaching you in public and from house to house, testifying both to Jews and to Greeks of repentance toward God and of faith in our Lord Jesus Christ." (v 18-21)

Paul's ministry to them is not a secret matter. It's public fact.

Paul has devoted himself to the church in Ephesus for a period of three years (v 31) doing at least three things:

1. Serving the Lord in humility (v 19)

2. Boldly teaching publicly and from house to house (v 20)

3. Preaching the gospel of repentance and faith (v 21)

This is the character of Paul's work among the Ephesian elders, and he can confidently say that he has been faithful in his ministry among them.

Paul's style of leadership provides a helpful and desperately needed **paradigm** for Christian leaders in the 21st century. Leading in ministry involves backroom vision-casting and executive leadership. So leadership is not less than that, but it is also more. Ministry also consists of service, teaching the saints, and preaching the gospel of repentance. In essence, Christian ministry must be about people and bringing them to Christ. Paul's ministry, furthermore, exuded humility. Paul knew the sinful life he had lived prior to meeting Christ and how he was "unworthy to be called an apostle" (1 Corinthians 15:9). Paul did not serve to advance his own fame. He served in ministry to ensure that God's grace toward him would not be in vain. Paul pressed on toward the upward call of God in Christ. He lived every moment of his life so that he might be able to say, "I worked harder than any of them, though it was not I, but the grace of God that is with me" (1 Corinthians 15:10).

We also see in his ministry the boldness to teach "anything that was profitable" (Acts **20:20**). A horrific temptation has poisoned so many pastors who compromise or minimize profitable teaching that seems unpalatable to so-called modern sensibilities. Indeed, this has been a problem of epidemic proportions since long ago, as far back as the age of the prophets. Micah said, "Thus says the LORD concerning the prophets who lead my people astray, who cry 'Peace' when they have something to eat, but declare war against him who puts nothing into their mouths" (Micah 3:5). True ministry, however, does not capitulate to the whims of the cultural mood. Western Christianity suffers from too many churches that preach a half gospel, which is no gospel at all. Pastors must be willing to imitate Paul. We must stand upon the sure and lasting rock of the infallible word of God. Upon that rock, we cannot and must not waver.

> True ministry does not capitulate to the whims of the cultural mood.

Finally, we see in the content of Paul's ministry among the Ephesians an emphasis on the gospel of repentance from sin and a summons to faith in the Lord Jesus Christ (Acts **20:21**). In this respect Paul preached the exact same message to both Jews and Gentiles. There is one gospel by which we are saved (see Romans 1:16).

Today, some Christian circles aim to modify this gospel. A proponent within this movement might claim that Jews, Muslims, and Christians worship the same God. This simply is not true. Christians are the only ones who worship the one true God—the God of Abraham, Isaac, and Jacob. Paul makes it explicitly clear here, even in this brief description of his message, that he testified that Jesus Christ must be believed upon for salvation. Jesus himself said the same thing to the Pharisees: "You know neither me nor my Father. If you knew me, you would know my Father also" (John 8:19). Jesus explicitly teaches that to reject him is to reject the Father. Paul does not modify the content of his message to suit the preferences or sensibilities of his audience. He boldly testifies the full gospel of repentance and faith.

The Innocent Watchman

Having begun his farewell by reminding the elders about his ministry among them, Paul uses formal language to solemnize the occasion in their mind. Even though they do not know it, Paul knows that he will not return to them. He knows that his return to Jerusalem will culminate in his imprisonment and persecution. He does not know the details, but he knows what awaits him (Acts **20:22-23**).

Why is Paul bent on going to Jerusalem? First, he is "constrained by the Spirit" (**v 22**). Paul understands his position before the eternal God. Throughout his letters, he describes himself as a slave and servant of God. He expects to suffer greatly, yet nothing will stop his journey because the Spirit of God compels him and constrains him. Paul will seize every opportunity "to testify to the gospel of the grace of God" (**v 24**). The mission he has received from Jesus Christ motivates him to action.

Second, Jerusalem is central for Paul because of its significance in the life of the early church. While Jerusalem was the birthplace of the church, persecution and the execution of the apostle James meant that the locus of church leadership and population quickly shifted to Antioch. Jerusalem quickly became home to the rejection of the gospel and a danger to the Christian movement. To proclaim the name of Christ in Jerusalem was tantamount to signing your own death sentence. Paul, however, does not press toward Jerusalem in order to self-destruct. He feels bound by the Spirit. There's also a missiological purpose to his travel. In terms of his ministry, the preaching of the gospel to the glory of God is everything to Paul. He measures the worth of his life by what-ever purpose God will use it for.

Knowing that he will never see the Ephesian elders again (**v 25**), Paul wants to charge them to persevere in the ministry with the same boldness that he has shown. With the weight of the farewell clearly to the fore, he makes a bold declaration: "I testify to you this day that I am innocent of the blood of all, for I did not shrink from declar-ing to you the whole counsel of God" (**v 26-27**). It is an astonishing statement. Again, Paul is referencing Ezekiel 33:1-7, where the Lord tells Ezekiel that he will serve as a watchman, speaking the oracles of God to warn the people (see page 78 and comments on Acts 18:6). If the watchman speaks and the people do not listen to the warning, the blood will be upon the people's heads. If the watchman does not speak, however, and the people are killed, the blood is on the watch-men's heads. Paul is saying that wherever he has been, he has not shrunk back from declaring the oracles of God to whoever would listen. Whether in Galatia, Philippi, or Athens, he preached the gospel. Whether before Festus, Felix, or the Praetorian Guard, Paul will preach the gospel. He preached publicly and house to house, which allows him to say that he is innocent of blood.

A good deal of preaching today is not innocent of blood. If you were to weigh many preaching ministries, they would prove to be severely lacking. The messages might be well constructed, with good literary form, conversational, and relevant. Many of them, however, are hollow and devoid of the gospel. In some cases, a church might actually preach the gospel but fail to proclaim the full counsel of God's word. Some preaching fails to make explicit the implications of the gospel's teachings or, even more dangerously, ignores parts of (or the entirety of) the Old Testament, effectively treating it as useless for the Christian life. Paul's preaching, however, thundered forth with unquestionable power and authority precisely because he proclaimed the gospel in its entirety. Paul can say that he is innocent of blood because he "did not shrink from declaring to [his listeners] the whole counsel of God" (Acts **20:27**).

Though Paul is addressing a group of church leaders, his words have significance for all believers. Paul knew that on judgment day he would not meet any Ephesians who could charge him with failing to tell them of the gospel. Paul says his hands are clean because he proclaimed the truth to everyone the Lord brought to him. Will we be able to say the same on the day of judgment?

Pay Careful Attention

Since Paul will not see these men again, he has a purposeful message for them the details of which form a comprehensive charge to undertake gospel ministry. Paul unabashedly held to these details in his own ministry as an apostle. He wants the Ephesian elders to be sober-minded watchmen over the people of God.

He says, therefore, "Pay careful attention to yourselves and to all the flock, in which the Holy Spirit has made you overseers" (**v 28**). Paul typically uses military **metaphors** to describe pastoral ministry (see 1 Timothy 1:18; 6:12; 2 Timothy 2:2-3). Here, however, he evokes Jesus' imagery and self-description. Jesus called himself the good shepherd and his disciples his sheep. The Ephesian elders, as the overseers of the Ephesian church, bear the responsibility for King Jesus' flock. Paul heightens the seriousness of the charge with the reminder that the sheep cost Jesus his very life (Acts **20:29**). The Ephesian elders, and all ministry leaders today, therefore, must heed this sobering call. If you are called to ministry, God places the care of his blood-bought people in your hands. Your task as a ministry leader must be to guard the sheep, love them, and lay your life down for them.

Paul continues by highlighting things he believes the elders must keep in mind. Paul warns them, "After my departure fierce wolves will come in among you, not sparing the flock; and from among your own selves will arise men speaking twisted things, to draw away the disciples after them" (**v 29-30**). Paul reminds the elders that some in this world zealously seek to destroy the church of God. First, there are "savage wolves." These are the external threats to the church.

The word "savage" indicates a malevolent, murderous intent. Their attempt to annihilate the church of God will not be a subtle one. The other threat is more insidious and difficult to spot—an internal threat of false teaching that subtly works to lead the sheep astray. Therefore, Paul exhorts the Ephesian elders to "pay careful attention" (**v 28**).

These threats haven't vanished in our own day. Pastors must still be ever vigilant to protect their flocks. Pastors can better guard their flocks by following Paul's example in the deep heartfelt care that he undertook as a church-planter, missionary, and pastor (**v 31**). Paul's life exuded an ardent desire for the glory of Christ. So his ministry embodied the hallmark of Christian humility, the power of Christian preaching, the robustness of sound theology, and tender Christ-like love. Ministries, and ministers, must aim at Paul as their model.

Paul concludes by commending the elders to God and his grace (**v 32**). Paul knew that his own strength could not guarantee the Ephesian elders' ministry success. Leadership in ministry recognizes the inability of human strength to produce supernatural results. The Holy Spirit, not Paul, had ultimately called these Ephesian elders as the leaders in that congregation (**v 28**). Paul certainly had a hand in modeling for them the content of ministry during his three years in Ephesus. For him, however, the ministry was empowered by the gospel, and these elders needed to be reminded that God's hand and grace would be the primary means through which they would succeed.

As Paul finishes his address, he makes a final defense of his ministry (**v 33-35**). This should be read as a postscript of sorts, which highlights the authenticity of his message. Paul didn't preach the gospel for selfish gain or ambition. He was controlled by one reality: the glory of God. This is not to say that ministers of the gospel should not be paid. In many places throughout the New Testament, Paul spills a lot of ink defending his right to receive financial support from the church (see 1 Corinthians 9:3-12; 1 Timothy 5:17-18). What he does here is to contrast himself with some of the false teachers operating throughout Macedonia and Asia who preached for selfish gain. Paul worked for his own money. Moreover, he worked in order that he might have something to give to the needy (**v 35**). Paul yearns for the elders of Ephesus to work hard for the glorious purpose of displaying love through generosity Thus, he reminds them of the words of the Lord: "It is more blessed to give than to receive."

A Tearful Goodbye

The mutual love of the Ephesians and Paul took a very tangible form in Miletus. Luke captures the emotion of Paul's departure. The scene is striking. Paul kneels with the elders and prays with them (**v 36**). The words recorded in **verse 37**—the "weeping," embracing, and kissing—denote the strong, felicitous bonds which united these men in godly brotherhood. The Ephesian elders were sorrowful because they would never see their elder brother and close mentor in the Lord in this life again (**v 38**). Loyal until the end and not desiring a premature departure, "they accompanied him to the ship."

Paul's impact on this church's life cannot be overstated, and the affections they had for him are demonstrable proof of that relationship. The ministry of any pastor will leave a lasting impact on the life of the church. Caring for the flock is stressful work, but a pastor who endeavors to minister according to the pattern of Paul among the Ephesians can usually enjoy an equal measure of affection and respect. More importantly, and by God's grace alone, the pastor who longs to minister as Paul ministered will not have worked in vain. When this life of labor ends, servants of Christ who lived as Paul did will walk into that celestial gathering and hear those resplendent words, "Well done, good and faithful servant" (Matthew 25:21).

Questions for reflection

1. As a Christian, what would you like your legacy to be, in your family, church, and community? How are you working toward that end?

2. Think about ministries that you are involved in. How do Paul's priorities here shape your priorities in those ministries?

3. In what ways do your pastors and elders live out the model of church leadership that Paul details here? What could you do to express your gratitude to them for those things?

8. THE RETURN TO JERUSALEM AND THE ARREST OF PAUL

In Acts 21, Paul's ministry takes on a different character. The beginning of this chapter concludes Paul's third missionary journey and begins the final phase of his life. Here, Paul reaches Jerusalem and begins his new ministry of defending his faith while on trial.

The Spirit Leads

Paul is on a mission to arrive in Jerusalem prior to Pentecost (20:16). Luke continues to describe the journey there in the beginning of this chapter. Paul and Luke left the Ephesian elders and travelled on a ship—most likely a small cargo ship—along the coastline (**21:1**). After a few stops, they then proceed to take a larger cargo ship southeast toward the region of Phoenicia (**v 2-3**). The ship docks in Tyre for seven days. During this week, Paul and Luke spend time fellowshiping with Christians already in the city (**v 4a**). Luke provides an interesting detail about Paul's stay in Tyre, writing that the believers "through the Spirit ... were telling Paul not to go on to Jerusalem" (**v 4b**).

We already know the Spirit is leading Paul to Jerusalem (20:22-23), but now these Christians seem to be proclaiming a different message from the Spirit. How do we make sense of this? Does the Spirit contradict himself? It seems that the Holy Spirit revealed Paul's future destiny of arrest and suffering to these Christians, just as he had to Paul. These Christians, therefore, did not announce a new, contradictory revelation of the Spirit. Instead, they attempted to persuade Paul to avoid the Spirit's leading into suffering. Thus, the Spirit had revealed to the disciples in Tyre what would happen to Paul: he would indeed suffer. The disciples, however, tried to dissuade Paul from proceeding and, inadvertently, encouraged Paul to oppose the Spirit's leading. Paul, though, committed himself to the will of God and the leading of the Spirit—even if that would lead him to tribulation. And so the believers at Tyre knelt down, prayed, and said their goodbyes to Paul and Luke as they boarded another ship (**21:5-6**).

Suffering for the Glory of God

Paul and Luke traveled to Caesarea and stayed many days with Philip, who was one of the seven **deacons** previously mentioned in Acts (**v 8**, see 6:5). While staying there, Paul and Luke encountered some prophetesses and a prophet. Philip had four unmarried daughters who prophesied (**21:9**). But there was also a prophet who visited, named Agabus (**v 10-11**). In the early church, prophecy took two forms, and both forms are found in this passage. First of all, prophecy can function as evangelism. Oftentimes, the act of teaching or sharing the gospel is referred to as prophesying. This form of prophecy is probably the one that Philip's daughters practiced. Philip is referred to as "the evangelist" (**v 8**) and his daughters most likely had the same ministry.

The second form of prophecy was literal prediction of near future events. This is seen most clearly in the character of Agabus. Agabus prophesied of Paul's future imprisonment in Jerusalem by the Jews and his eventual handing over to the Gentiles. He took Paul's belt and bound his own feet and hands to represent Paul's impending imprisonment (**v 11-12**). Agabus, whose prophetic voice had already benefitted the early church (11:28), now confirmed the same future for Paul that the Christians in Tyre had been told about by the Holy Spirit.

In **21:12**, Luke records that he himself and the people in Caesarea urged Paul not to go to Jerusalem. But Paul, as he had done before, declared his intent to press on toward certain persecution and showed willingness to even die for the sake of the gospel. Paul desired above all else to lift high the name of Christ (**v 13**). Those present with Paul, knowing that they could not change Paul's mind, proclaimed, "Let the will of the Lord be done" (**v 14**). Luke, Paul, and a few companions then made their way to Jerusalem (**v 15-16**).

We can learn something revolutionary from Paul: fully aware of the impending suffering to befall him, he did not hesitate to continue on his mission. His chief concern in life was not comfort, safety, or a long life. His chief purpose, rather, centered on the proclamation of the gospel of God, whatever the cost. God summons all his people to trust perfectly in his will. Indeed, the suffering that Paul faced in his earthly life brought much glory to God. Paul's sufferings also bore tremendous fruit as his tribulations often resulted in the advancement of the gospel and the kingdom of God. In the Christian worldview, therefore, the question should not be "Why does suffering happen to me?" but rather, "How can I proclaim the gospel of Jesus in the midst of my trials?"

Pursuing Unity through the Gospel

The Jewish leaders in Jerusalem welcome Paul and his travel companions as they arrive in the city (**v 17**). Paul's travel companions were Christians from Asia Minor and thus were Gentiles. For them to be welcomed by these Jewish believers reveals the impact of the Jerusalem Council in Acts 15 and the unifying power of the gospel. One of the chief leaders from that council was James, the half-brother of Jesus. James became the leader of the church in Jerusalem following the persecution that caused many disciples and believers to disperse. Here in Acts 21, Paul meets James and the elders of the church (**v 18**).

Paul reports to the elders in Jerusalem and tells them "one by one the things that God had done among the Gentiles" (**v 19**). Essentially,

Paul took these men through a travelogue from his third missionary journey to the Gentiles. And at the beginning of **verse 20**, the elders respond by glorifying God for the ministry to these Gentiles. Prior to Paul's missionary journeys, the Jews, did not consider the possibility that these Gentiles would be part of God's kingdom. But now the Jewish leaders praise God for the extent of his salvific work. Only the gospel could bridge the ethnic divide which existed between Jews and Gentiles. Only the gospel can tear down the dividing walls which exist in our own day. Only the power of the cross can unite the voices of Africans and **Caucasians** as one people praising God together.

> Only the gospel can tear down the dividing walls which exist in our day.

After Paul's retelling of his journey, the elders then turn their focus toward the relationship of believing Jews and the law. In the last half of **verse 20** the elders remind Paul of the thousands of Jews who have trusted in Jesus Christ for faith since Pentecost. It is as if they are saying, *Paul, it is wonderful that God is calling so many Gentiles to faith. But do not forget about the Jews!* For there are many Jews, both believing and unbelieving, who are curious about Paul's teaching regarding the law. There are many Jews who believe in Jesus who are still "zealous for the law." Also, many Jews believe that Paul teaches antinomianism—that he wants to abolish the Law of Moses (**v 21**). The elders in Jerusalem understand that a misunderstanding of Paul's teaching could lead to a fissure in the already fragile bonds between Jews and Gentiles. Thus, they ask in **verse 22**, "What then is to be done?"

The relationship between a believing Jew and the law is a biblically complicated issue. On the one hand, the Jewish believer cannot find salvation in the Jewish traditions. On the other hand, Scripture does not forbid Jews to continue their practice of Jewish customs. It is best to understand this issue in specific contexts. This is an issue of local adaptation for Jewish Christians. They can integrate themselves into the lifestyle of the Gentiles while having a respect for their own Jewish history. They can also continue in Jewish customs but with the understanding that salvation comes through Christ and Christ alone. The elders, therefore, wanted to cautiously keep the gospel at the forefront of these Jews' lives, while respecting their individual consciences.

In order to best maintain unity, the elders ask Paul to listen and adhere to their plan of sponsoring the purification of four men under the Nazirite vow (**v 23-24**). These four men are Christians who still live under their vows as Nazirites. Numbers 6:1-13 explains the contours and character of this vow. A Nazirite pursued a purified, holy lifestyle of single-minded devotion to God. This means the vower must avoid wine, dead bodies, and anything unclean. What is important for our discussion is that there were Christians in the New Testament age who still continued in this Jewish custom. These elders, understanding how many could misconstrue Paul's teaching (to guard against which they had sent the circular letter in Acts 15, that they now remind Paul of in **21:25**), asked Paul to take part in this purification ceremony and deflect any charge of opposing the law (**v 26**).

Paul could have denied the request of the elders. However, in humility he submitted himself to the elders' request because he highly prioritized maintaining the character of the gospel while also promoting the unity of the church. He did not want to leave an obstacle between the gospel and the Jews in the city. Paul did not give up on the central affirmations of the gospel by his submission to Jewish customs. He continued to preach Jesus Christ for the forgiveness of sins. The gospel cannot change, but our presentation of it, at times, must. Paul models to us the act of "becom[ing] all things to all people" (1 Corinthians 9:22).

Paul's character throughout Acts shows believers today something astounding about true freedom. Paul knows the freedom he now has as a child of God. Indeed, in Galatians 5:1, Paul exclaims, "For freedom Christ has set us free". Believers, however, can let freedom assume the status of an idol and, consequently, enslave themselves to freedom. We can easily entrench ourselves in our own freedom and thus paralyze our ability to serve others. True freedom, as Paul demonstrates, means we can dispense with our own preferences, wants, and needs. True freedom is a freedom from self. Freed from selfishness, Christians can lay down their own desires as a sacrifice on the altar of Christian love. Paul, though free from the law, made himself a servant of the law in order to love his brothers and sisters in Christ. That is true Christian liberty.

Beaten and Arrested

Though Paul took part in the purification of these Nazirite men, non-believing Jews stirred up a mob to attack him (Acts **21:27**). They accused Paul of being "against the people and the law and this place" (**v 28**). They seem to have assumed that Paul had brought a Gentile named Trophimus into the inner-sanctuary of the temple (**v 28-29**). The inner sanctuary was off-limits to non-Jews. But, as **verse 29** explains, this was not a fact but was a false accusation. Paul was with Trophimus in Jerusalem, but he knew not to bring a Gentile into the temple. The accusation, however, was enough to spark a violent riot.

The mob intended to kill Paul right there on the spot (**v 30-31a**). The Roman tribune, however, heard of the uproar and brought soldiers with him to stop the madness (**v 31b-32**). A tribune was a commander of up to 1,000 soldiers. The soldiers' speedy response to the uproar was due to the location of their watch tower. Herod the Great had built the Tower of Antonia at the northwest corner of the temple to keep careful watch over the crowds. As the tribune came near, the crowd ceased their abuse of Paul. Mass confusion continued as the tribune sought an explanation for the unrest (**v 33-34**). In order to sort the matter out and to calm the crowd, the tribune arrested Paul and managed to bring him to the barracks (**v 34**), despite the murderous intent of the mob (**v 35-36**).

The tribune was surprised to hear Paul speak in Greek (**v 37**) and then assumed that Paul was the Egyptian perpetrator who in AD 54 led a revolt in Jerusalem (**v 38**). Paul responded by identifying himself as a Jew from Tarsus. Interestingly, Paul made a request. He desired to speak to the mob who had just attempted to kill him (**v 39**). The tribune gave him permission, and Paul walked back out to the crowd (**v 40**) to give a speech that would certainly not be forgotten.

Questions for reflection

1. Is there a person in your life you have neglected to tell the gospel to due to a fear of rejection or pain? Pray for boldness.

2. How does Paul's example of faithfulness to Christ in the face of upcoming persecution encourage you in your life?

3. "We can easily entrench ourselves in our own freedom and thus paralyze our ability to serve others." This is hard to see in our own lives, but can you spot areas in which you are most tempted to idolize your freedom or preferences? What would it look like to worship Christ in those areas instead?

PART TWO

The violent mob in chapter 21 becomes Paul's audience in chapter 22. His message to them is one of truth and also grace. As we will see, Paul's words fall on deaf ears and hardened hearts.

Paul's Life Before Christ

Paul begins his speech by addressing the Jewish people as brothers and fathers (**22:1**). This expresses Paul's desire to respect the crowd, despite the manner in which they have acted toward him. As Paul begins to speak, the crowd hushes in silence (**v 2**). Why? The text says it is because Paul is speaking in the Hebrew language. Though Roman guards surround Paul, his mind is set on the Jewish people. Paul continually assesses how he can steward his circumstances toward gospel proclamation. No matter what trials he faces, his mind focuses upon his calling to preach Christ and Christ crucified.

Paul begins to share about his life. He shares three things from the biography of his life before meeting Christ: where he comes from, who he learned from, and what he sought to accomplish. First, Paul introduces himself as a Jew born in Tarsus, Cilicia (**v 3**). Though he was born in this Mediterranean coastal city, Paul attributes his formation to his upbringing in Jerusalem. In this first part of his biography, Paul shows that he too knows this city. He too is a Jew. But, as we will see later, Paul has shifted his primary identity away from Judaism to Christ.

Second, Paul shares who he learned from during his time in Jerusalem. Paul sat under the instruction of Gamaliel, one of the most prominent Jewish teachers of the day. Paul describes his Jewish education by stating that he studied "according to the strict manner of the law of our fathers" (**v 3**). Paul took the Jewish law seriously.

Third, Paul shares what he set out to do in his life as an educated Jew. He sought to persecute those who subscribe to the "Way" (**v 4**). The Way was a common label used of Christians in the early days of the church (Acts 19:9; **22:4**; 24:14). Paul sought to both imprison and kill men and women of the Way (**22:4**). If Paul had stopped his speech at this point, the crowd would have applauded. Paul, however, no longer rooted his life in his ethnic identity, education, or work. Something powerful and transformative had gripped Paul as he traveled on the road to Damascus to persecute Christians (**v 5**).

Paul's inclusion in his speech of his life outside of grace should encourage Christians to reflect on their own lives before Christ. Believers who can remember coming to Christ in repentance and faith should look back on their previous life of total sin and rebellion. This recollection should stir up our affections for God and cause us to respond in thanksgiving. Only as we acknowledge the depth of our sin can we appreciate the glory of our conversion (1 Timothy 1:15). Furthermore, Paul, by sharing about his life before meeting Christ, allowed his story to demonstrate the transformative grace of the gospel.

Paul's Encounter with Christ

Paul begins to expound upon what is recorded in Acts 9. On his way to persecute Christians, a blinding light shone upon Paul (Acts **22:6**). But beyond this light was a voice that asked, "Saul, Saul, why are you persecuting me?" (**v 7**). Paul notes that the arresting party with him saw the light but could not understand the voice of Jesus (**v 9**). Interestingly, likewise the mob present before Paul here sees the light of the gospel but fails to understand its saving power. **22:10-13** continues the recitation of his conversion found in Acts 9. He traveled as a blind man to meet Ananias, at which point his sight was restored.

In **22:14**, Paul interrupts his testimony of Acts 9 with a declaration of the gospel. He shows that Ananias, a devout Jew, was the instrument God used to point Paul to the gospel and the mission field. Ananias says, "The God of our fathers appointed you to know his will, to see the Righteous One and to hear a voice from his mouth" (**22:14**). Ananias tells Paul that the God he has studied under Gamaliel is the same God whom he has encountered on the road to Damascus. This amounts to an astounding revelation for Paul. He now comes to terms with his real encounter with the eternal God—with Yahweh himself. For it was God's will to reveal himself to Paul: that he would "see the "see the Righteous One" as he saw and heard the Jesus whom he persecuted. This "Righteous One" was prophesied in Isaiah 53:11, which both Paul and his Jewish audience would have known. So, at that moment in Acts **22:14**, Paul declares before the mob what Ana-nias declared to him years previously: Jesus is God.

Not only that, but "the God of our Fathers" (that is, Abraham) sent Jesus to Paul so that Paul might become a witness to all people (**v 15**). Paul finishes this part of his speech by showing that his faith was to be clearly expressed in baptism (**v 16**). Paul publicly identified himself with Christ through baptism, and he continues to do so now through his declaration of the gospel to the Jews. Though our lives will surely not have the global impact of Paul's, we too share in Paul's testimony. We too have been saved by God out of our sin, rebellion, and disobe-dience. God longs for his people to demonstrate the transformative power of the gospel through baptism and evangelism.

Paul's Mission from Christ

Paul continues to declare what happened after his encounter with Jesus. He recounts that during prayer a trance fell upon him (**v 17**). In this trance, Jesus appeared to him again and commanded him to leave Jerusalem quickly because some Jews, like those in the audience, re-jected his new life and sought to kill him (**v 18**). Paul responds by say-ing, "Lord, they themselves know that in one synagogue after another I imprisoned and beat those who believed in you. And when the blood of Stephen your witness was being shed, I myself was standing by and approving and watching over the garments of those who killed him" (**v 19-20**). Paul raises with God his doubts about the nature of his mission. He knows what he has done. He knows that even though he is now a child of God, his newfound brothers and sisters in the faith will fear and not trust him. God confirms his mission for Paul, saying, "Go, for I will send you far away to the Gentiles" (**v 21**). By saying this,

God promises his preserving power over Paul and the presence of his providential hand over Paul's life.

Before we observe the reaction of the Jewish mob before Paul, we must note the progression of Paul's speech. He began by addressing the crowd as brothers and fathers (**v 1**). He then began to speak in the Hebrew dialect (**v 2**). He confirmed his utterly Jewish identity by highlighting his hometown, his education, and his zeal for the law (**v 3**). He then described his hatred for Christ-followers and his well-known reputation for being the persecutor of the Way (**v 4-5**). He then began to slowly change the tone of the message as he described his encounter with God on the Damascus road (**v 6-11**). Though in our eyes Paul has clearly revealed that Jesus is God in this account, the Jewish crowd apparently continue to listen because they remain ignorant of this. Paul continues by revealing that the Righteous One commissioned him for this mission.

Up to this point, the Jewish mob, though they may be disturbed or annoyed, has not reacted aggressively against Paul. It is as if Paul has not said enough yet to make their accusations against him credible. The last sentence of his speech, however, tips the scales and elicits violent aggression against him. In his last sentence, Paul, in effect, announces that the grace and goodness of God has extended to the Gentiles. The crowd can listen no longer. They have heard enough. Paul is declaring that even Gentiles are part of God's family. The Jews cannot stomach this thought because they revile the Gentiles. They view the Gentiles as defilers of the temple, and as harsh overlords. The Jews in Jerusalem repudiate Gentile rule of their holy City of David. Now, however, Paul tells them that Yahweh has had the "audacity" to graft the Gentiles into the family of God.

Today, many teachers of the Bible try to change the message of the gospel to make it less offensive. The gospel, however, is always offensive. In Acts 17, Paul knew he would lose many in his audience by speaking of the resurrection from the dead. Here, in Acts 21 – 22, Paul knew that he would elicit a strong response from the Jews by proclaiming the inclusion of Gentiles in the kingdom of God. Paul could have left out these points which caused so much hostility and mockery from the crowds. He could have avoided speaking of the resurrection from the dead as he preached at Mars Hill. He could have spoken like a "good Jew" in Jerusalem and not have mentioned the Gentiles at all. For Paul to do that, however, would have meant giving up on the central doctrines of the gospel and their implications. He would have been attempting to shape God to the culture, rather than summoning the culture to turn to God. The idea of conforming God to our cultural ideals remains tempting. Adapting the doctrines of the gospel to today's culture might lead to less suffering and mockery for Christians. To do that, however, would mean jettisoning the gospel and the message of salvation. If your desire for cultural relevance supersedes your theological commitment to the Christian faith, then you will not preach good news, though you might proclaim culturally popular news. Christians must know how the gospel offends the most deeply-held assumptions and values of any society, so that we are prepared to challenge the culture when the gospel does offend.

Paul: The Roman Citizen

In his account of this situation, Luke makes the consequences of Paul's speech crystal clear. He writes, "Up to this word they listened to him" (**22:22**). After Paul announces that the Gentiles are fellow recipients of the gospel, the mob return to their violent anarchy. They shout at the Roman guards to take Paul away and kill him. Their shouts and requests should remind us of the same sort of crowd before Jesus and Pilate who shouted, "Away with this man" (Luke 23:18).

The Roman tribune orders his men to take Paul into the barracks, away from the mob (Acts **22:23-24**). The tribune's whole task in this courtyard is to keep the peace. He accomplishes this at first, by allowing Paul to calm the crowd with his speech. But once the speech shifts toward the inclusion of the Gentiles, the crowd revolts once again.

Thus, the tribune's move to escort Paul away from the crowd is nothing more than attempting to regain peace.

The tribune orders Paul to be examined by scourging. The tribune functions like a police officer in attempting to gather the facts of what has transpired. At this time, it was thought that the most effective way to obtain the truth was to beat a suspect with a strip of leather laced with stone. Why does the tribune beat Paul and not individuals in the rioting crowd? He does not speak Hebrew and thus has not understood any of Paul's speech. He acts on what he has observed. Paul has apparently insulted the crowd so severely that they desire him to be killed. Paul appears to be in trouble here as the tribune's soldiers tie him up to whip him (**v 25**).

Paul, however, interrupts this procedure with a shocking question which stops the persecutors in their tracks. He asks, "Is it lawful for you to flog a man who is a Roman citizen and uncondemned?" (**v 25**) Now the tribune has an even bigger problem: he has instigated the illegal torture of a Roman citizen. When the centurion reports Paul's question to him (**v 26**), the tribune is understandably confused and asks Paul if he truly is a Roman (**v 27**), for this man speaks in

> Paul would endure any suffering which befell him; but he did not pursue unnecessary suffering.

the Hebrew dialect and bears little physical resemblance to a normal Roman. Paul confirms his citizenship and explains that he was born a Roman citizen (**v 28**). At this, the tribune is afraid and releases Paul from torture (**v 29**). The protection of Caesar extended to every citizen of the Roman Empire. Paul trusted in the will of God and would endure any suffering which befell him. He did not, however, pursue unnecessary suffering. Suffering for the sake of suffering does not glorify God. Paul used his citizenship as a protection not because he feared suffering, but rather, as a gift of God that enabled him to continue to advance the gospel.

We can rightly deduce the providential hand of God over Paul's status as a Roman citizen. God sovereignly orchestrated the background and events of Paul's life so that he might acquire the status of a citizen of the empire and thereby enjoy the protections of the empire as he sought to preach the gospel throughout the world. The birthplace of Paul, therefore, was no mere coincidence. His status as a Roman citizen was a visible representation of God's control over every facet of his creation.

Luke then records that on the very next day, the tribune brings Paul before the chief priests and council. The tribune continues his investigative work as he tries to deduce the "real reason" for the accusations levied against Paul (**v 30**). The chief priests represent the **Sanhedrin** of the Jewish people. This council is the same one that previously interrogated Jesus Christ, Peter and John, and now they do the same with the Apostle Paul.

Paul is seated before the council to give an answer for the accusations before him. But before we look at those in chapter 23, it is important to point out Paul's missiological mind. In 20:16, we read of Paul's persistence in traveling to Jerusalem. He had a sense of urgency. We can understand that better now. How else would Paul have had the opportunity to declare the gospel directly to the Sanhedrin? He could not do that from Philippi, Corinth, or Ephesus. He could only do that in Jerusalem. Despite the many trials and suffering that it took for Paul to arrive here, he has finally made it. Here stands Paul, servant of Christ, before Roman and Jewish leaders. His weapon? The gospel of our Lord Jesus Christ.

Questions for reflection

1. What is your story of conversion? How can you speak about it in a way that makes much of Christ, rather than focusing on yourself?

2. Paul was rescued from torture here by his providential birth as a Roman. Where in your life has God's providence been clearest to you? In what ways are you using any privilege you have to serve Christ?

3. Paul saw every place he went to as an opportunity to preach Christ, and no problem or weakness as an excuse not to. What would change in your life if you adopted that mindset?

9. ON TRIAL FOR THE RESURRECTION

Acts 23 begins with Paul's trial before the Sanhedrin. Paul's ministry to the Gentiles stood at the center of the controversy surrounding his preaching. As the chapter unfolds, we see that this is what Paul must also address before the Sanhedrin. Paul's own life hangs in the balance—his answers could mean life or death. He stands trial not just to defend his theology but to be judged as to whether or not he should be executed. This is the drama of Acts 23.

As we so often see throughout Scripture, however, this chapter reminds us that God often flips the script on our expectations. Like Jesus before the authorities in the Gospels, the interrogated becomes the interrogator. The Sanhedrin will not judge Paul; God will judge the Sanhedrin. As the narrative progresses in the next several chapters, Luke reveals that nobody interrogates the gospel—rather, it is the gospel which interrogates all who hear its words of **conviction**.

As Wise as a Serpent

Paul begins his testimony before the Sanhedrin by declaring his innocence (**v 1**). Then the scene takes a physical turn when the high priest Ananias commands that Paul be struck on the mouth (**v 2**). Ananias probably understands Paul to be claiming that he, though a Christian convert, still serves Yahweh and lives as a faithful Jew. For Ananias the two identities—Christian and Jew—are incompatible. Thus, Paul's words are tantamount to blasphemy in the view of Ananias.

Paul retorts bitterly with sharp words in **verse 3**. Why did he respond with such venom? Indeed, a wide chasm of disparity separates the trial narratives of Jesus before the Sanhedrin and Paul here in Acts 23. Jesus responded to his accusers with calmness and silence. He spoke only a few words. Paul, however, pulls no punches and lashes out against the high priest—though he apparently did not know it was the high priest who ordered his mouth to be struck (**v 4-5**). This scene raises a litany of questions. First, was Paul right in his bitter response? It appears that Paul himself realizes he has lost his temper, as he indirectly apologizes in **verse 5**. Second, how on earth could Paul not have known that the high priest had given the order?

Luke does not offer an explanation. He does not comment on Paul's actions. Luke takes a page out of the playbook of a historian who seeks to retell the facts as they are: no more, no less. We are left to surmise. On the one hand, we could look at Paul's actions as sinful. Jesus remained silent during his trial and told his disciples that "to one who strikes you on the check, offer the other also" (Luke 6:29). We could say Paul lost his temper and that this is behavior we should not seek to emulate when called to give a defense of the gospel. On the other hand, Jesus himself used harsh language when speaking to the Jewish leaders, even the Sanhedrin. Indeed, Paul's language here bears a resemblance to Jesus' words in Matthew 23:27, when he said, "Woe to you, scribes and Pharisees, hypocrites! For you are like whitewashed tombs..."

When presented with a difficult interpretive decision, oftentimes the simplest explanation offers the safest route. Most likely, Paul did lose his temper and lashed out in a moment of frustration. He believed he had been severely mistreated and he let his audience know it. Once told whom he was addressing, Paul offered an apology, grounding his confession not in the character of Ananias but in the Old Testament Scriptures.

Whichever reading is correct, it leads us to what Paul does next—he masterfully redirects the proceedings. Paul recognizes the makeup of his audience. Half are Sadducees, the other half Pharisees (Acts **23:6**). These two groups had sharp disagreements about the Jewish religion. The Pharisees taught a more conservative understanding of the law and held all the books of the Hebrew Scriptures as authoritative. Furthermore, they believed in a resurrection from the dead. The Sadducees, conversely, only held Genesis to Deuteronomy as authoritative and denied a bodily resurrection. Paul exploits this disparity and declares that he stands trial because he holds to the hope of the resurrection of the dead. His words function like tinder and gasoline on an already smoldering fire. The assembly erupts as the two competing worldviews clash (**v 7-8**). The disagreement culminates when the Pharisee party declares Paul's innocence of all charges (**v 9**). The scene ends with the tribune intervening by having Paul taken and removed from the situation (**v 10**).

> Paul's words function like gasoline on a smoldering fire.

This section provides a parable for our modern times. Many opponents of Christianity today highlight the innumerable **denominations** and **sects** which exist in the church. The charge goes something like this: "How can Christians lay any claim to the truth if they themselves have divided so many times and cannot present a united message?" The scene in Acts 23, however, is a reminder that opponents of Christianity often disagree within their own camps on issues of truth, too. The charge can easily be turned back on those who so confidently level it at the Christian faith. Left to ourselves, humanity will never think and act in a way in accordance with the truth. Only through God's grace and God's revelation—which comes from outside of humanity and was **incarnated** in humanity—can humanity know the truth and embody the truth. Christians, like all humans, sometimes disagree, but Jesus is the Truth (John 14:6). We must look to the Word to discover the truth.

Paul's actions reveal the prudence of discernment and acting wisely in difficult circumstances. In using his knowledge of this audience, Paul shifted the focus of the trial from his faith to their doctrinal divisions. With one swift comment, Paul redirected the attention of the entire proceedings. Paul no longer stood on trial. He had taken the conversation into a deeply theological and significant doctrinal matter. Christians can learn from Paul in these proceedings. Through a simple question, we can shift conversations from an assault on Christian teaching to the hearts and worldviews of those to whom we speak.

Protection Promised

That night, when Paul is alone, unsure of his future, and perhaps entertaining thoughts of fear and anxiety, the Lord visits the apostle with words of comfort. God says to Paul, "Take courage, for as you have testified to the facts about me in Jerusalem, so you must testify also in Rome" (**v 11**). Notice the intimate language. The Lord came and "stood" by Paul. God knows Paul's state and how the circumstances Paul faces could begin to hinder his faithfulness. Jesus comes by his side with words of comfort and settles Paul by explaining the will of God. God is not done with Paul. Paul has more to proclaim and more people with whom to share the gospel.

Paul not only needed comfort; he needed courage. For Paul to face the road ahead of him, he needed the courage that only God can supply. Christians, likewise, need courage to stand, to proclaim, and to declare the glory of God in the midst of this crooked and twisted generation. That kind of courage can only come from God himself. When pressed with doubts, fears, and anxiety, grab hold of God and do not let go. Plead with him for courage and strength. Confess your weakness and inability, and run to the God who can and will provide.

Verse 11 sets the direction for the rest of the book of Acts. God has revealed to Paul that he intends for him to go to Rome and to present the gospel to the emperor himself (**25:11-12**). The rest of the narrative will demonstrate God's faithfulness in carrying Paul through various trials to his final destination. It will also highlight how Paul continues to press on in faithfulness and maintains his courage as he trusts in God and his promise. We, likewise, must press on in faithful obedience to God, just as Paul did. God has revealed the destination of us all. He has revealed the eternal glory which awaits his household of faith, his people. He has pulled back the curtain of eternity and shown his children the celestial gathering that awaits them. We, therefore, must always strive to keep the promises of God before us, that we might press on in faithful obedience and live boldly for the cause of Christ.

Protection Delivered

The next section chronicles a failed conspiracy to kill Paul. In **23:11**, God has promised his protection and revealed his plan to take Paul to Rome. Now, he delivers on his promise. Nothing will thwart God's will. No man, no plan, and no plot can hinder the all-powerful God from accomplishing his purposes. When the world seems to have turned against the people of God and the flames of persecution burn, we can still know that God reigns.

Here, a band of Jews make a pact not to eat or drink until they have accomplished their mission to kill Paul (**v 12**). **Verses 13-15** give the details of the conspiracy. The chief priests will request Paul's presence before the Sanhedrin. En route, a mob of forty men will ambush Paul and beat him to death. But somehow Paul's nephew hears of the plot and rushes to tell Paul of his impending doom (**v 16**). The apostle immediately calls for a centurion who accompanies Paul's nephew to the tribune (**v 17-21**). Upon hearing the news, the tribune dismisses Paul's nephew and begins planning for Paul's safety (**v 22-23**).

The tribune, Claudius Lysias, recognizes that he must get Paul out of Jerusalem before Paul is murdered. Claudius knows that Paul's Roman citizenship affords him the right to access the Roman legal process. Jerusalem, and the volatile situation erupting there, is clearly no place for Paul to get the trial he deserves. So Claudius hatches a plan to get Paul from Jerusalem to Felix, the governor, in Caesarea.

Claudius' Appeal to Felix

Claudius plans to have Paul sent away under cover of darkness (**v 23**). (The third hour of the night would have been midnight, according to the way time was thought of in the first century.) The point is that Paul is smuggled out of Jerusalem in the dead of night. And not only that, but two hundred soldiers, seventy horsemen, and two hundred spearmen are to escort him. The situation in Jerusalem is so severe that the rescue of the apostle requires Rome to deploy a formidable convoy to protect him.

That Claudius decides to send Paul to Felix, the **procurator** of the Judean province, shows something of the seriousness of Claudius' concern. Claudius would not have sent Paul to Felix if he could have handled the situation himself. The severity of the situation, however, demanded that a higher authority get involved (**v 24**). So Claudius sends Paul to Felix, along with a letter explaining Paul's plight (**v 25**).

Written in perfect Greek, Claudius' appeal is an absolute masterpiece of letter-writing. The letter's opening line shows that first-century letter-writing style differed from today's format (**v 26**), in that whereas today we end our letters with the name of the writer, in the first century, Romans started their letters started with the name of the writer.

As the body of the letter unfolds, we see that Claudius is a typical self-preserving bureaucrat. Claudius informs Felix that he rescued Paul, a Roman citizen, from a bloodthirsty mob of Jews who were about to kill him (**v 27**). Claudius, of course, does not reveal the whole truth here. He doesn't mention that he did not learn of Paul's citizenship until he had given the order to have Paul arrested and flogged, which actually violated Paul's rights as a Roman citizen. He only recounts that he realized that Paul was not guilty of anything deserving death, and that the dispute had to do with Jewish, and not Roman, law (**v 29**).

Luke is contrasting the self-serving soldier and his half-truthful letter with the Christ-exalting apostle and his fully truthful testimony.

Even though Claudius is guilty of manipulating the truth and putting himself in a more favorable light, his actions and the letter he writes put into action the official legal process for a Roman citizen, which is what he details in **verses 28-30**. At this point, Claudius is following Roman protocol. He appeals to Felix to serve as the judge of a Roman citizen whom he is legally required to protect.

Paul's military escort takes him as far as Antipatris, a Roman military outpost, which was about sixty miles (97 km) northwest of Jerusalem (**v 31**), and about three-quarters of the way to Caesarea. The foot soldiers stay the night, and then return to Jerusalem after sending Paul and the horsemen on their way to Caesarea (**v 32**).

When they arrive in Caesarea, Paul and the letter are handed over to the governor (**v 33**). Upon reading the letter and perceiving that Paul is no criminal, Felix asks Paul what province he is from (**v 34**). Why does Felix care about Paul's province? Because the closer you get to Rome, the closer you get to Caesar, and the closer you get to Caesar, the more complicated the political situation is likely to be.

Paul informs Felix that he is from Cilicia, which is closer to Rome than Caesarea, and too close for Felix to feel comfortable—and so he assures Paul that he is going to receive a fair trial and will be protected in Herod's **praetorium** (**v 35**). (Herod's praetorium had been built by Herod the Great and functioned as the governor's palace.) Paul should have been set free on account of his Roman citizenship, but Felix decided it was best for Paul to await his hearing under the protection of Felix's own guards.

The Jewish plot did not surprise God. He knew exactly what would happen and, before they even hatched their plot, had already curtailed their efforts. As the narrative unfolds, God's providential protection continually guides Paul along his journey to Rome. The road of God's providence may contain much difficulty, but we walk along it with God. The path of discipleship will come with pangs and sorrow, trials and suffering—but it is a glorious way that leads to the celestial city of God and to hearing those longed-for words, "Well done, my good and faithful servant."

Questions for reflection

1. When you are talking with non-Christians about the gospel, how could you gently and respectfully point out the contradictions, divisions or weaknesses in the worldview they are espousing?

2. While the details of 23:11 were specific to Paul, how does what it reveal about God encourage you today toward continuing to seek to share the gospel with those around you?

3. How and when are you tempted to speak in half-truths, leaving out uncomfortable parts of the truth? What would it look like to tell the whole truth, and nothing but the truth?

PART TWO

The Apostle on Trial

The news of Paul's detention in Herod's praetorium reached the Jews in Jerusalem. Ananias, the high priest, arrived to make his case against Paul (**24:1**). Ananias is a very complicated figure. He was appointed in AD 47 and was known for having an explosive temper. He was deposed by King Agrippa in AD 59 and murdered by Jewish assassins six years later. He was horribly unpopular with the Jews, but he was still the chief priest, and the fact that he shows up to prosecute the case against Paul sends a strong signal. It would be the equivalent of the president of the United States showing up to prosecute a trial taking place in the Supreme Court.

Before arriving in Caesarea, Ananias hires an attorney named Tertullus to be his spokesperson in the courtroom (**v 1**). Tertullus knows how to handle himself in the courtroom and proves to be an articulate attorney. Ananias bears a symbolic presence, as the one bringing the charges against Paul; Tertullus, however, will serve as his mouthpiece.

The Apostle Accused

Tertullus' purpose in his opening lines is simple: to massage and pamper the Roman governor Felix (**v 2-3**). He shamelessly flatters Felix. Imagine a prosecutor in an American courtroom saying, "Judge, I don't know of any more significant judge than you. Under your jurisdiction, justice has been promoted, crime has come to an end, and peace has come to our nation." Yet everything Tertullus says about Felix is a lie. Felix's regime was one of the most corrupt and incompetent to ever rule in the name of Rome. During his tenure, peace was the last thing Judea enjoyed. Roving bands of insurrectionists constantly wreaked havoc in Judea, assassinating Roman soldiers and Roman citizens. And every reform he sought seemed to have been aimed at increasing his own personal gain. Felix was a spectacularly crooked governor. Yet that did not stop Tertullus!

After the false compliments, Tertullus makes three statements of false accusation against Paul. First, he casts Paul as a plague on the region (**v 5**). Paul has spread the disease of dissension. In the Roman world, threats to stability were feared more than anything else because Caesar needed stability for the Roman Empire to thrive. If Paul has acted seditiously among the Jews, Rome cannot afford to let him go free—he is a liability.

Second, Tertullus charges Paul with being "a ringleader of the sect of the **Nazarenes**." Framing Paul as the leader of the Nazarenes' sect is Tertullus' attempt to cast Christianity in terms not of a religious faith but a fanatical political party. At the time, political sects which were really just rebellious groups of bandits terrorized the region. Essentially, Tertullus equates Paul and the sect of the Nazarenes with radicalized insurrectionists. This kind of accusation against Christians has been made before in Acts (21:38), indicating that the temple authorities constantly sought to slander the church as a group of dissenting Jews who threatened not only the Jewish faith but the peace of Rome.

Finally, Tertullus claims that Paul "even tried to profane the temple" (**v 6**). Roman law, more or less, afforded Jews the right to execute persons for desecrating the temple. Roman governors had no interest in getting involved in Jewish religious problems, so if the Jews found someone guilty of temple desecration, the Romans would look the other way. The Jews, however, had been spectacularly unsuccessful in pressing this charge against Paul. That does not stop them from trying again before Felix, this time through the silver-tongued lawyer Tertullus.

Verse 7 presents a textual problem. That's because it does not appear in many translations. The passage is preserved in the **Western Text**, but relegated to a footnote in other texts. Some scholars omit the verse, believing that scribes added it to better connect **verse 6a** to **verse 8b**. Others include it, arguing that the context points to Claudius Lysias as the person to be questioned by the governor (**v 22**). While the passage does present a rather curious textual variant, it ultimately does not obscure the clarity this section of Scripture (nor undermine the **inerrancy** of the Scriptures).

In **verse 8**, Tertullus says, "By examining him yourself you will be able to find out from him about everything of which we accuse him." In this conclusion to his opening statement, he hopes to bring Paul under the direct examination of the governor himself. Tertullus believes that if Paul falls under the scrutiny of Felix, then Paul will falter, and the case will be won. But Tertullus is oblivious to the divine hand of God at work in every detail, and now overseeing his apostle's defense.

The Apostle's Defense

After the other Jews affirm the accusations laid out by Tertullus (**v 9**), Felix gives Paul the opportunity to respond (**v 10**). Paul's opening lines to Felix are in stark contrast to Tertullus' greeting. Rather than resort to flattery, Paul simply states the facts about Felix's rule. He stands confidently on the solid ground of the gospel, which is why he can make his defense cheerfully and with integrity.

Paul's defense is brilliant. In **verse 11**, he begins to dismantle each of Tertullus' accusations. In all likelihood, when Paul mentions the "twelve days" here, he is referring to the total amount of time he spent in Jerusalem until his trial before Felix. In other words, Paul ridicules Tertullus by using the simple fact that twelve days cannot afford even the most charismatic of leaders the opportunity to stir up a great deal of dissension and sedition. Indeed, the Jews, when they first found Paul, found him in no dispute with any person in Jerusalem (**v 12**).

Paul then puts Tertullus and the Jewish leaders on the defensive by claiming that the burden of proof falls on them to substantiate the charges (**v 13**). He openly, and cheerfully, testifies to being a Christian, and he firmly grounds the roots of his faith in the Jewish Scriptures (**v 14**). And, far from being a political sect, Paul says that Christians are committed to following the way of the Lord—that is, "the Way" is a way of spiritual reform, not of political subversion.

Paul's defense should remind all believers of the absolute necessity of the Old Testament Scriptures. Paul roots his identity as a Christian in the foundation of the Hebrew texts, which expressed an aching for and pointed toward the day of Jesus Christ. The Old Testament contains the promise of God to his people. The very foundation of Jesus' ministry flows from the pages of that sacred text, where God appeared with fire on the mountain, where God pronounced through his prophets the coming day of his Son; and where God enshrined his promises for all generations everywhere. Without the Old Testament, there would be no Christian faith.

In **verse 15**, Paul theologically strips Ananias and the other Jewish leaders naked before Felix. Paul is being cleverer than may immediately meet the eye, for Ananias was a Sadducee (and the Sadducees did not believe in life after death, and so rejected the doctrine of the resurrection) but clearly at least some of the elders who had come with Ananias (**v 1**) "themselves accept[ed]" the "resurrection of both the just and the unjust" (**v 15**). Paul appears to be identifying and widening this theological faultline among his accusers. They are divided over the notion of a future resurrection for judgment—for Paul and the other apostles, Jesus' resurrection from the dead was proof of it (17:31), and was fundamental to the Christian faith. Christ's resurrection came as the first of many in the eternal family of God.

> Christ's resurrection came as the first of many in the family of God.

Therefore Paul locks his eyes on eternity, which is why he cares so much about the purity of his conscience before God and men (**v 16**). **Verse 16** is a restatement of the same words he spoke before the Sanhedrin a few days earlier (**23:1**). Paul can say that his conscience is clean because he always strives to fear God rather than men. He knows that he will one day stand before God to give an account for his life and conduct.

Paul states that he had been away from Jerusalem for a significant amount of time, but a short time previously had returned to present alms and offerings (**24:17**). His last visit had come five years earlier at the conclusion of his second missionary journey (18:22), but it had been nearly ten years since he had spent any substantial time in the city, at the Jerusalem Council (15:4).

Paul concludes his defense in **24:18-21**, once again seizing the opportunity to assert his innocence and to declare his hope in the resurrection of the dead. He challenges Ananias and the other Jewish leaders to speak and explain what Paul had done in violation of Jewish customs. Again, Paul's words before the Sanhedrin and his words here before Felix point to the theological issue at the heart of his disagreement with Ananias. Paul recognizes that this conflict has nothing to do with Rome and its peace; it has everything to do with those who believe the gospel and those who reject it.

The Apostle Under House Arrest

After Paul finishes his defense, Felix states that he will wait until Claudius Lysias arrives to decide Paul's case, which indicates that Claudius Lysias is not present at this trial (**v 22**). Interestingly, Luke tells us that Felix had a good working knowledge of Christianity—the gospel was not completely foreign to him. This is not surprising, since the gospel had already taken root in Caesarea decades before (10:44-46). In this small yet important imperial city, there are evidently enough Christians, perhaps even influential ones, that even the Roman governor has some knowledge of Christianity. And Felix knows enough to know that Ananias has come with a baseless accusation. From this point onward, the Jews have nothing on Paul. Paul's case simply becomes a matter of the Roman judicial process—exactly as God intended.

The scene shifts in **24:23**. Felix gives the order to keep Paul in protective custody in a safe place, probably still the praetorium. He is kept in custody—not necessarily as a criminal but for his own protection from the Jews. Felix gives Paul a considerable measure of freedom, so much so that his friends are permitted to come and meet his needs.

While he is in Roman custody, Felix and his wife, Drusilla, send for Paul to hear more about the Christian faith (**v 24**). Drusilla's father—a minor provincial king—promised her in marriage at the age of six to Epiphanes, the son of King Antiochus of Commagene. Drusilla was a Jew and Epiphanes a Gentile. In order to validate the marriage, Epiphanes needed to submit to the Jewish practice of circumcision, but he refused, so the marriage did not take place. When she was 14, Drusilla's brother, King Agrippa II, married her off to King Azizus of Syria. But Drusilla left Syria to marry Felix and become the wife of a Gentile, thus defying Old Testament law.

Despite all this, Drusilla shows an interest in Christianity and wants to hear from Paul. But as Paul preaches the tenets of the Christian faith, Felix is struck to the core and filled with fear at the thought of his coming judgment. Yet, rather than repent and trust in Christ, Felix dismisses Paul (**v 25**), and ends up summoning him periodically for the remainder of his two years in office only in hopes of receiving a financial bribe, rather than eternal truth (**v 26-27**).

Acts presents its readers with spectacular stories of conversions and repentance. Who can forget the turning of Saul to Jesus? How could the conversion of Cornelius pass away from memory into the recesses of history? The Philippian jailer fell before Paul and cried out for salvation. Acts demonstrates the power of the gospel to turn hearts of stone into hearts of flesh.

But at the same time, the Scriptures present this real and unembellished story of Felix's rejection of the gospel as a sobering reminder that those spectacular stories are not inevitable, or even the norm, when the gospel is preached. Luke is teaching us three significant things. First, Christians must unabashedly preach the gospel of Jesus Christ. The church stands upon the witness and testimony of the gospel's power to raise the dead to life. The preacher in the pulpit stands not in his own strength but ascends the steps (as it were) on the sure foundation of God's word. The Christian preaches and proclaims the gospel; it is God who saves. Second, preaching the gospel also means preaching conversion and a turning away from sin. Without repentance, the gospel is turned into a message of **cheap grace**. Obedience to God flows from a heart transformed by the gospel. Christian preaching is only Christian when it summons the dead to newness of life. Paul's message of righteousness and self-control challenged Felix and Drusilla because they lived entrenched in sin and disobedience—but the challenge needed to be made. Finally, rejecting the gospel by refusing to repent does not make it untrue. Rejecting the gospel and banishing the thought of judgment to the outer rim of your mind will not stop the coming day when Jesus Christ judges the whole earth. Judgment approaches. It will come swiftly. It will come unannounced. Will you be ready when the trumpets sound? And will you share the gospel until that time, undeterred by those who reject the message and cling to their sin?

Questions for reflection

1. What does Paul's defense teach you about how to respond to false accusations you might face for following Christ?

2. Why is the resurrection central to the message of Christianity? How central is it to your view of your own life?

3. In Acts 24, Paul operates out of a healthy fear of God, while Felix operates out of an unhealthy fear of man. Why is it liberating to live seeking the approval only of the Lord?

10. TO CAESAR YOU SHALL GO

In Acts 25, Luke never mentions the name of God. The hand of God, however, runs throughout the entire narrative. His providential hand orchestrates every event in this chapter. He protects his servant Paul and sets the apostle on a trajectory toward proclaiming the gospel before the most powerful and influential people in the empire. God may seem absent; indeed, it may even seem that God has abandoned Paul. His grace, however, continues to empower Paul and give him the wisdom and strength to meet his adversaries with poise, peace, and conviction. The promise of God to Paul in 23:11 directs and under-girds the entire narrative. God's promises will never fail.

Another Trial

Luke begins chapter 25 by introducing us to Felix's successor, Porcius Festus; and just "three days after Festus had arrived in the province, he went up to Jerusalem from Caesarea" (**25:1**). Festus came from a very different background than Felix. Festus was a blue-blooded Roman whose family had long been influential in the Roman Empire. Felix had left things in such a mess that Rome was, apparently, determined to send someone of noble pedigree to try to clean up the mess that had been made in Judea.

Luke shows us that Festus is immediately trying to establish a re-lationship with the Jews. He heads to Jerusalem just three days after arriving in Judea, which makes the statement that he is trying to bring peace, law, and order to the province.

Of all the things Festus might have had on his agenda on that visit, there was one topic that took precedence above all else for the chief priests and Jewish leaders: Paul. The Jews urgently "laid out their case against Paul" (**v 2**), which shows that he was the number one concern that they wanted to address with the new governor. Indeed, the Jewish leaders wasted no time in asking Festus, "as a favor against Paul that he summon him to Jerusalem" (**v 3**). At this point, Paul was in Caesarea, but the Jews were acting as if they wanted Paul in Jerusalem to hear charges. In reality, "they were planning an ambush to kill him on the way," which is reminiscent of the foiled plot in Acts 23. The Jews were trying to prey upon Festus' new role and his desire to appease the Jews.

Festus heard their pleas, but he informed the Jews that Paul would remain in Caesarea and that "he himself intended to go there shortly" (**25:4**). We might expect a new governor to be inclined to grant this favor to the Jewish authorities in hopes of establishing a good rapport. Indeed, Festus wants nothing more than law and order in his region. He has a job to do and an emperor to please. Festus, however, has a completely different outlook than Felix. Perhaps this is an opportunity to show the Jewish leadership this.

Festus appears to have a very clear view of the world in which he lives. He sees things through the lens of Roman rule. He places every person in one of two camps: Roman or not Roman. Because of Paul's Roman citizenship, Festus cannot imagine turning him over to the Jews. Instead, Festus offers this solution: "Let the men of authority among you go down with me, and if there is anything wrong about the man, let them bring charges against him" (**v 5**). Festus, therefore, intends to strike an authoritative balance. On the one hand, he seeks to appease the Jews by continuing the legal proceedings against Paul. On the other, he reminds the Jews of his power as their Roman governor.

Again, the Jews intended to precipitate Paul's death. Again, God would not allow it to happen. Indeed, rich irony permeates the story. By their actions, the Jews actually advanced the message of the gospel despite their violent opposition. Though Paul lived as a shackled, defenseless prisoner, the all-powerful God of the universe protected the apostle. It is better to live as a prisoner who belongs to Jesus than a free man without a relationship with God.

Stability Trumps Justice

After his first encounter with the Jews, Festus "stayed among them not more than eight or ten days" (**v 6**) before he went down to Caesarea. Governors typically liked being in Caesarea because it was the most Roman city in the area, and they did not enjoy being in Jerusalem—which shows that, in staying there more than a week, Festus indeed had some significant issues to address during his trip. The day after Festus arrived in Caesarea, "he took his seat on the tribunal and ordered Paul to be brought," and "the Jews who had come down from Jerusalem stood around him, bringing many and serious charges against him that they could not prove" (**v 7**). The tribunal was a very formal legal setting in which the governor would preside as judge and jury. The Jews, and Paul for that matter, needed to win Festus' backing, for his verdict carried the full weight of the law.

Luke details the severity of the charges laid at Paul's feet. At the same time, Luke also mentions the inability of the Jews to prove any of the accusations. The Roman judicial process required eyewitnesses and demonstrable proof, so that Roman citizens would be protected from baseless accusations. Time and again, throughout the book of Acts, God uses Paul's Roman citizenship as a shield to protect Paul as well as a conduit through which Paul could travel the Roman Empire.

Paul finally enters this portion of the narrative as he begins to provide his own side of the story: "Neither against the law of the Jews, nor against the temple, nor against Caesar have I committed any offense" (**v 8**). Paul mentions the Jews, the temple, and Caesar in his opening line of defense. This likely means the Jews had indicted Paul on charges involving each of these three categories. The Jewish leaders brought everything they could against him, in order to see Paul executed. They knew that they would have to do more than charge Paul with teaching erroneous doctrines in accordance with the Jewish faith. They needed to make him out to be a seditious charlatan. In other words, the Jews adopted a strategy in their accusations against Paul similar to the one they had used against Jesus. When the King of kings had stood in their presence, the Jewish people—the promised people of God—had exclaimed, "We have no king but Caesar" (John 19:15)! As they did with Jesus, so now they do with Paul: the leaders of Israel cast off their identity and seek to kill God's messenger.

Now Festus shows his true colors. Again, he concerns himself with regional stability, not justice. In an attempt to appease the Jews, Festus offers Paul the opportunity to go to Jerusalem and face trial (Acts **25:9**). Paul, however, emphatically reasserts his defense to Festus: "To the Jews I have done no wrong, as you yourself know very well" (**v 10**).

Oftentimes, believers will face similar opposition or mistreatment. Christians will come into contact with those who care nothing for righteousness or justice. Indeed, the cultural revolution aims at the dismantling of Christian beliefs and convictions in every corner of Western society. The cultural elites will not tolerate Christian theological and doctrinal fidelity. Festus cared nothing for Paul and his freedom, and only wanted to secure his own version of peace and prosperity. Christians today must prepare themselves for similar moves by governments and rulers who will happily sacrifice the Christian worldview and the freedoms of Christians upon the altar of the moral revolution.

I Appeal to Caesar!

After Paul asserts his innocence to Festus, he then says, "I am standing before Caesar's tribunal, where I ought to be tried" (**v 10**). The apostle reminds Festus that the governor is the representative of Caesar, judging the case of a Roman citizen. Why should Caesar hand his prisoner over to someone else? Paul's appeal to Caesar is one of innocence. He says, "If then I am a wrongdoer and have committed anything for which I deserve to die, I do not seek to escape death" (**v 11**). Paul knows he has nothing to hide, and that if he has done nothing wrong, then no one, not even Festus, can hand him over to the Jewish leaders.

Notice Paul's judicial reasoning with the Jews and with Festus. One might think that as a Christian, Paul should simply remain silent. Indeed, during his trial, the Lord Jesus remained silent before his accusers. Why then did Paul defend himself? First, Jesus' silence before the Jews and Pilate was a matter of prophetic fulfillment. Isaiah 53:7 pointed to the suffering Messiah who would, like a sheep before its shearers, remain silent. Second, Jesus came for the single purpose of dying on the cross. He submitted to the will of the Father. He came in order to be the perfect sacrifice which would secure eternal atonement for the people of God.

> Paul did not defend himself to save his own neck, but to safeguard Christian witness.

Paul's situation, therefore, is set in an entirely different context than that of Jesus. Paul defended his credibility and innocence as a matter of highlighting before rulers and opponents the purity of Christian character. Indeed, in the first centuries of the church, the church **apologists** pointed to the virtuous character of Christians as a defense of the faith. There are ancient manuscripts from non-Christian rulers and governors which point to the sublime character displayed by Christians. Paul, therefore, did not defend himself to save his own neck. We know Paul's story and life—he was willing to die for the gospel. His defense was, rather, intended to safeguard Christian witness and promote Christian virtue. Believers today have much to learn from Paul in this episode. Believers should proclaim their innocence and point to the vitality of their living, but not as a motivation to save their own skin. Our motivation must be the purity of the gospel and of its message.

Paul concludes his testimony with four resounding words: "I appeal to Caesar" (Acts **25:11**). This was a legal formula of sorts, and it would circumvent much of the legal process. Any Roman citizen who faced charges of a capital offense could make an appeal to the Roman Emperor. By making an appeal to Caesar, Paul's case would go all the way to Caesar. There was therefore no verdict from Festus, and Paul was kept in custody, away from the Jews.

Make no mistake, Paul knew what he was doing, and that God had every detail under his sovereign control. God had revealed to Paul what he would do through Paul's testimony. God intended for Paul to stand before governors and kings and proclaim the excellency of Christ. Throughout this narrative, Luke never mentions God. Yet God certainly is at work as he executes his will around and through Paul.

Indeed, as the story unfolds throughout the rest of Acts, Luke presents the reader with the way in which God uses this seemingly calamitous event to continue to spread the gospel throughout the world. Paul would testify before a king. Paul would exemplify the light of Christ to a crew on a ship which was sailing for Rome. Paul would work powerful miracles before the inhabitants of an island. Paul would encourage disciples in Rome. Each and every one of these events happened because God had his hand on Paul. The remaining narrative demonstrates that Paul's situation in no way surprised God or caught God off guard. The sovereign Lord over the universe had planned every detail of Paul's life. He would accomplish his purposes. Nothing will ever stand in the way of our God.

After Festus hears Paul's appeal, he confers with his counsel on how to proceed. He comes back and says to Paul, "To Caesar you have appealed; to Caesar you shall go" (**v 12**). Festus may have realized that there was nothing supporting the accusations that the Jews had made against Paul, but after this appeal his verdict would have to wait. Paul now had to go to Rome to stand before the Emperor of Rome.

This first part of Acts 25 continues to reveal the folly of the hard-hearted Jews who continue to oppose the message of the Messiah. The narrative also, in an inconspicuous way, glories in the providence of God. As Paul stood on trial, he continued to trust in God and believe in his sovereign plan. Today, as Christians, we will meet opposition and persecution, and face accusations. We will stand trial in the cultural courts of modernity and **postmodernism**. The high priests of the moral revolution will charge us with heresy and **sedition**. They will indict us for holding antiquated beliefs which oppose the new post-Christian status quo. Indeed, Western culture views Christian **dogma** as diametrically opposed to its vision of progress. The question, therefore, is this: are we, as God's people, willing to give an answer for the hope that is within us (1 Peter 3:15)?

Questions for reflection

1. In what way does stability sometimes trump justice in your own society? And in your own life?

2. What can you learn from Paul's behavior in the face of hateful accusations?

3. What difference does it make to know that every apparently unpredictable twist and turn of life is in fact under the Lord's sovereign control?

PART TWO

The second part of Acts 25 introduces a lengthy section of narrative in which Paul gives his testimony before King Agrippa. Much as in the first part, Luke does not mention God in these verses. Despite this omission, Luke clues the reader in on a conversation between two secular rulers in which the providence of God can clearly be seen. God has worked Paul's situation perfectly. Paul's lifetime of faithfulness and God's gracious hand have brought Paul to a crucial moment in his ministry: he will proclaim the gospel before a king.

Enter the King

Acts **25:13** introduces us to Agrippa the king and Bernice, his sister. This pair were involved in one of the most infamous incestuous relationships in ancient history. It was a matter of imperial concern and a scandal in Rome. The Emperor Claudius had ordered Bernice to marry (someone besides her brother, obviously), but she almost immediately left her marriage (to a man named Polemo) to go back and live as her brother's queen.

Now Agrippa and Bernice show up, most likely to pay respects to the new governor. Their timing, however, is no accident. God has brought these two rulers to Caesarea at the perfect time. Luke tells us that Agrippa and Bernice stayed in Caesarea for many days, and during this time, "Festus laid Paul's case before the king" (**v 14**) so that Agrippa might have a better understanding of this problem that Festus had inherited from Felix's reign. Festus recounts the events that had taken place with the chief priests and the elders of the Jews in Jerusalem (**v 15**), and then he begins to explain how the situation had escalated (**v 16-17**). He informs Agrippa of the urgency of the matter: "I made no delay, but on the next day took my seat on the tribunal and ordered the man to be brought" (**v 17**). Festus clearly takes this matter very seriously, presumably because of the threat it poses to regional stability. Perplexed by the situation, Festus seeks the assistance of the king and his sister to help him determine the matter.

Lessons from a Conversation

As Festus continues, his words begin to demonstrate the divergence between his expectations as the region's new governor and the reality of what he has inherited from his predecessor. He tells Agrippa, "When the accusers stood up, they brought no charge in [Paul's] case of such evils as I supposed" (**v 18**). Festus must have expected the Jews to accuse Paul of egregious acts against both the Jews and Rome. Instead, the new governor tells Agrippa, "they had certain points of dispute with [Paul] about their own religion and about a certain Jesus, who was dead, but whom Paul asserted to be alive" (**v 19**).

You can almost sense the puzzled tone in his voice as Festus relays this information to Agrippa. This case presents Festus with a perplexing and complicated set of doctrinal disputes which lie outside his realm of expertise. Indeed, he perceives the heart of the matter to surround this man named Jesus, who apparently had died but who, Paul believed, had risen from the grave. Paul was not charged with any treasonous crimes against Rome; he was charged with holding a view about this man Jesus that many of the influential Jews disagreed with.

This portion of the narrative provides profound insight, as it reveals the relative ignorance of the gospel among Roman leaders. They may have heard of the gospel (as Felix clearly had), but they did not understand it. The Jews viewed Jesus as the perpetrator of a great scandal which had disrupted their entire religious culture. For the Romans, however, the tale of Jesus only led to confusion. Yet we must not miss what happens here in Acts 25: Roman rulers discuss the resurrection of Jesus! This scene depicts two non-Christian leaders pondering the theological glory of Jesus' resurrection from the dead. God has started to prime their hearts for what will come in chapter 26.

Moreover, this episode shows believers the importance of a faithful gospel witness. When Christians share the gospel, they might hope to see a person repent and believe on the spot. Rarely, however, do such spontaneous conversions happen. Even if a Christian does share the gospel and a person repents instantly, that individual has probably benefitted from a long line of faithful gospel witnesses who have already shared with them the glories of Christ. Acts 25 reveals a conversation between two rulers who have *started* discussing the gospel of Jesus Christ. When you share the gospel, you may not see an instant conversion. You do, however, cast a seed which may germinate and take root later on when that person has another conversation about religion. You do not know how God can use a brief moment of faithfulness and implant his word in a person's heart.

As these two leaders discussed the resurrection of Jesus, they began to notice different distinguishing characteristics between the Jews and Paul. The Jews approached the situation in an unruly manner and accused Paul of wrongdoing based on specious evidence. Paul, however, remained humble and confident, and exuded a godly contentment during the course of his trial. Surely many who were watching this case unfold took notice of that stark contrast. As the story develops, the rulers of the secular world will peer into the world of Paul and glimpse and judge his character.

> We must not only proclaim Christ; we must live as Christ.

In the same way, the world watches us and our actions today. The behavior of the body of Christ can either bear tremendous fruit among nonbelievers or harm the witness of the gospel. Hypocrisy will kill the credibility of one who proclaims to follow Christ. As Paul stood trial, he not only needed to stand on truth; he needed to live the truth. We must not only proclaim Christ; we must live as Christ. We summon others to repentance; we must live holy lives. Indeed, as Peter says in 1 Peter 2:12, "Keep your conduct among the Gentiles honorable, so that when they speak against you as evildoers, they may see your good deeds and glorify God on the day of visitation."

Living a holy life does not remove the possibility of people in our culture accusing Christians of wickedness—indeed, in some cases, living a godly life will invite accusations of wickedness. The darkness hates the light. 1 Peter 2:12 therefore reminds believers of the future hope of obedience. The world may accuse us today of wickedness. God, however, on the day of judgment, will vindicate his people and will receive glory from our godliness today.

The comments of Festus also reveal the confusion which shrouds the resurrection. That confusion extends into every age of human history. But while confusion and even ridicule surround Jesus' resurrection, Acts 25 shows how Christians can steward that confusion toward spiritual conversations and gospel opportunities.

In Chains, but Not Captive

Festus is so confused about how he ought to deal with Paul's case that he tells Agrippa he is "at a loss how to investigate" the matter that is causing such problems with the Jews (Acts **25:20**). Finally, he tells Agrippa that Paul has been ordered to be held until he can be sent to Caesar (**v 21**). Now King Agrippa is curious—he wants to see and hear from this controversial figure for himself (**v 22**) rather than just take Festus' word for all that has unfolded. Perhaps, being a Jew himself, Agrippa wants to use this opportunity to see if he might be able to come to a better understanding of the controversy than Festus.

The pace at which events transpire demonstrates how consuming this matter must have been for all of the parties involved. Luke writes that "on the next day Agrippa and Bernice came with great pomp, and they entered the audience hall with the military tribunes and the prominent men of the city. Then, at the command of Festus, Paul was brought in" (**v 23**). It is worth envisaging in our mind's eye the assembly gathered together to hear Paul, and realizing what God has done. The governor, the king and queen, the military tribunes, and the leaders of the city have gathered together to hear about and from this man named Paul. God has assembled a congregation of interested men and women, many of whom presumably think they will come and see this Paul made a mockery. What they will receive, however, is a powerful, bold, and glorious presentation of the gospel of Jesus Christ. The unsuspecting congregation assembles, believing they hold the power and authority. Soon, a man in chains will appear before them. Ironically, it is only that man who is truly free, and he possesses the key which could set the entire room free: not from Roman law but from the wrath of God.

We must remember the power of the gospel which God has given us through our salvation. The chains and shackles of this world cannot hold any Christian captive. Believers in Jesus Christ live in the freedom of the gospel, with their hearts and minds set on the eternal kingdom to come. The world will continually believe it has the upper hand— that it possesses power and wisdom. Fallen and hardened human hearts will look upon the Christian gospel with contempt and scorn. As the guards dragged Paul into the room and before the assembly, no doubt everyone there saw him in light of his chains. Paul, however, marched into the room knowing his freedom. He had been set free from the chains of sin and death.

Once Paul was brought in, Festus said, "King Agrippa and all who are present with us, you see this man about whom the whole Jewish people petitioned me, both in Jerusalem and here, shouting that he ought not to live any longer" (**v 24**). Festus does not employ **hyperbole** to describe the situation. In a straightforward manner, he describes the hatred the Jews had for Paul and the desperation of Paul's situation. Despite the many accusations, Festus had found "that [Paul] had done nothing deserving death" (**v 25**), but he decides to send him to Caesar after his appeal.

Most of Festus' introduction serves as a summary of what we have already read in Acts 25, but the context matters greatly. The Roman Caesar at this time was Nero, a ruler known for his brutality and intolerance of any disruption. In this scene, Festus attempts to wipe his hands clean of the issue by giving the Roman citizen Paul the appeal he has requested. There have already been two conspiracies to murder Paul, so this must seem like a much wiser option for the new governor than handing Paul over to the Jews.

Festus continues by admitting his lack of clarity on the case, saying, "I have brought him before you all, and especially before you, King Agrippa, so that, after we have examined him, I may have something to write. For it seems to me unreasonable, in sending a prisoner, not to indicate the charges against him" (**v 26-27**). Festus basically concludes by asking for help in defining the charges against Paul. He has spent a good portion of his time as governor dealing with this issue, yet he still has no real clarity as to why Paul is in this situation. Even Paul may not have known exactly why God had placed him in this predicament. He did, however, trust in a providential God. He did know the power of the God he served. He trusted the will of God and met every trial with faithfulness and conviction.

Paul's exemplary character serves as an encouragement to each generation of Christians. He knew the hope of the crucified and resurrected Christ, even as it seemingly stirred up hatred or confusion in those around him. The gospel of Jesus Christ is no less a scandal today than it was during Paul's imprisonment—a beautiful scandal that ought to be shared with unabashed passion, whatever the consequences. For from this gospel comes an incomparable gift.

Questions for reflection

1. What does this section teach us about God's sovereignty?

2. How do we respond humbly when we are accused as Christians of being both out of our mind and too clever?

3. Why was Paul able to be unintimidated as he stood before the elites of his society? How can those same truths help you to live with courage today?

11. THE APOSTLE AND THE KING

Chapter 26 contains the entirety of Paul's defense before King Agrippa. As has been noted before, writing letters in the ancient world bore a significant cost. Each and every word here, then, has a cost associated with it. For Luke to record this message in full means he viewed it as a significant moment in his narrative and necessary for the health of the church.

A Life Transformed by the Grace of God

The chapter begins with Agrippa allowing Paul to make his defense. Paul stretches out his hand and begins his speech (**26:1**). The imagery Luke employs shows the seriousness of Paul's message. Paul did not stretch out his hand because he liked to use hand gestures when he spoke, but to demonstrate to his audience the gravity of what he was about to say.

Paul begins with profound humility. He expresses gratitude that he has the opportunity to make his defense before King Agrippa (**v 2**). He reveals that even when before secular rulers, Christians must show honor and respect. Then, in **verse 3**, Paul pinpoints Agrippa as his audience of one. Though a host of people populates the room, Paul directs his energy and attention to this one man. Paul knows the opportunity that God has given him to share the gospel with a man of great authority and power. Even in a moment of great stress and anxiety—indeed, a moment where his life is on the line—Paul stands ready to present the truth of the gospel.

A Jew Among Jews

Paul begins his defense with his personal testimony. Believers too, therefore, should not underestimate the power of personal narrative in sharing the gospel. Indeed, telling others of God's saving work in our lives connects nonbelievers to the gospel in a powerful way. Sharing your testimony will not only communicate the truth of Christ but show his grace as it worked on you.

Paul reveals that the Jews know his manner of life (**v 4**). Indeed, he recounts the prominent nature of his upbringing. He was no mere Jewish boy. His parents saw to it that Paul would receive the strictest and most conservative teaching available to a Jew—and he became a Pharisee (**v 5**). Then, in **verse 6**, Paul does something amazing. He says, "And now I stand here on trial because of my hope in the promise made by God to our fathers." In other words, Paul condemns the Jews who have accused him of abandoning the Jewish faith. In his eyes, he is *more* Jewish than his accusers because he recognizes that God's promised Messiah has indeed come. Paul grounds his identity in the promises of God made to his ancestors, which were fulfilled in Jesus Christ.

In **verse 7**, Paul highlights the absurdity of the charges laid against him. In his eyes, Jews have accused him for being too Jewish because he believes God has actually fulfilled his promises. **Verse 8** details his ridicule for those Jews who believe Paul to be a madman for proclaiming that God raised Jesus, a dead man, from the grave. As he says, "Why is it thought incredible by any of you that God raises the dead?" After all, this was the promise made in Scripture by God. Paul is pointing out that resurrection is consistent with Jewish beliefs. In this way he turns the tables on his accusers who ridicule his belief in the resurrection. Why should Jews exhibit surprise at Paul's message of the resurrection of Jesus when the Hebrew Scriptures point to such a resurrection?

Paul then shifts his story and points to his own previous skeptical beliefs about those who followed Jesus. Indeed, Paul believed he possessed a calling from God to persecute Christians, who dared to worship this Jesus of Nazareth (Acts **26:9**). He would once have identified himself with those Jews who now condemn him and ridicule his beliefs. Paul recounts his life as a persecutor of Christians and his hatred for the message of the gospel when he worked for the chief priest and approved the execution of Christians captured by Jewish authorities (**v 10**). With zeal and fury, he had assaulted Christians and even tried to trap them with charges of blasphemy (**v 11**). With a masterful flare of rhetoric, he builds anticipation in his audience. How could Paul, a persecutor of Christians and agent of the Jewish elite, now stand condemned by those very authorities? What has happened in Paul's life to radically alter his course?

The Unmatched Power of Jesus

Paul's story continues as he retells the facts of his Damascus excursion. He set out under the authority of the high priest to persecute Christians and to bring them back to Jerusalem for imprisonment (**v 12**). Then there comes the cosmic plot twist. A light, brighter than the sun, shone around him, and he fell off his horse (**v 13-14**). He heard a voice that said, "Saul, Saul, why are you persecuting me? It is hard for you to kick against the goads" (**v 14**). A goad was a very sharp stick used by a plowman to prod a sluggish ox into moving faster. When Jesus said "It is hard for you to kick against the goads," he meant, *What in the world do I have to do to get your attention, Paul?* This remark reveals that Jesus had been at work in Paul's life for a long time. Jesus had been prodding Paul toward himself throughout his life. Paul, however, "kicked against the goads": he had, in futility, attempted to resist the power of Jesus Christ.

But there on the road to Damascus Jesus gripped Paul's heart and immediately drew him out of the kingdom of darkness. Paul's conversion was radical. One minute he was setting out to persecute the people of God. The next minute he belonged to that very family. Paul's conversion, however, though glorious and radical, bears a resemblance to every conversion of every person who has placed their faith in Christ. One minute we were living as enemies of God, servants of Satan, and children of wrath (Ephesians 2:4). Then, at the moment we placed our faith in Christ, God delivered us from the kingdom of darkness and transferred us into the kingdom of his beloved Son (Colossians 1:13). In conversion, children of wrath become children of the living God.

At the same time, as sudden as Paul's conversion may seem, Jesus' comment, "It is hard for you to kick against the goads," reveals God's providential hand over the entire span of Paul's life. The glorious and gracious God of the universe providentially orchestrated the story of Paul's conversion. His hand rested on Paul even when Paul lived as his enemy. When Paul approved of Stephen's stoning, God prodded Paul closer to salvation. When Paul cast his vote for the murder of Christians, God was there, working in Paul's heart. Paul resisted, but God pursued. In the same way, we have each rebelled against God. We have sinned against him. We have rejected him. We have hated him. But the One whom the nineteenth-century poet Francis Thompson called "the Hound of Heaven," our gracious God, pursued us despite our sin. Indeed, "while we were still sinners, Christ died for us" (Romans 8:5). Paul's conversion—and your conversion—was no accident. Conversion is a culmination—the culmination of God's saving plan for you, which he purposed before the foundation of the world.

If God's will beats the drum of your life and has led you to that moment of saving faith, then every moment of your life bears an eternal significance. Suffering, trials, pain, darkness, depression, sickness, and even a life engrossed in the vilest of sin all shaped you, led you toward conversion, and became gospel gems in your testimony. Indeed, Acts 26 reveals the power of a gospel testimony. Paul enjoins his listeners to behold the unmatched power of Jesus Christ, who has ruled over every minute of Paul's life and who saved Paul from his hell-bound journey.

Additionally, Paul's testimony should influence the prayer life of Christians. As believers, we can and should pray for our non-believing family members and friends—that the goads would be too sharp and prove too exhausting for them to continue to resist. Christians can pray that God would use life's circumstances as a means to draw people to repentance and to show their need for Jesus Christ.

As the narrative continues, Paul draws his audience into the vision he saw on the road, and names the source of the voice thundering from the light. Jesus spoke from the light, identifying himself as the risen King of kings and also identifying himself with his church (Acts **26:15**). Here, Paul gives more details of his encounter with Christ than are found in Acts 9—he recounts that Jesus said to him, "Rise and stand upon your feet, for I have appeared to you for this purpose, to appoint you as a servant and witness to the things in which you have seen me and to those in which I will appear to you" (**26:16**). Jesus informed Paul that he would now live as a servant of Christ, not as a persecutor of Christ. Jesus' transformative power in the heart of Paul provides the only explanation of how a leading agent of the high priest, bent on stamping out the Christian faith, could then become the church's greatest missionary, evangelist, and theologian. God does not merely convert people; he commissions them.

> God does not merely convert people; he commissions them.

In **verse 17**, Paul tells of how Jesus told him that he would send Paul to Jews and Gentiles as an ambassador of the kingdom. Why? So that Paul might "open their eyes, so that they may turn from darkness to light and from the power of Satan to God, that they may receive forgiveness of sins and a place among those who are sanctified by faith in me" (**v 18**). This verse details the spectacular glory of the gospel. Three particular phrases deserve special attention.

1. "Open their eyes ... turn from darkness to light." Without Christ, all remain spiritually blind. Sin and death shrouds the eyes of sinners in a thick darkness which nothing but the power of Christ

can dissipate. Left to our own devices, we will wander in the darkness and remain in our sin. Even more problematically, many nonbelievers do not even realize that they wander in the blackest night of sin and despair. That is why Jesus sent Paul—and sends all his people—equipped with the gospel of grace to open the eyes of the blind and turn them from the darkness to the resplendent light of Christ. Indeed, we sing of this enlightening power of the gospel in this timeless hymn:

> *Amazing grace! How sweet the sound*
> *That saved a wretch like me!*
> *I once was lost, but now am found,*
> *Was blind, but now I see.*

This, indeed, is the power of the gospel: the lost are found and the blind see.

2. "Turn ... from the power of Satan to God." This phrase exposes the repugnancy of wandering in darkness. Spiritual blindness is not morally neutral. Paul, recounting the words of Jesus, reveals that those who wander in blindness serve Satan. Paul makes this clear in Ephesians 2:1-2: "You were dead in the trespasses and sins in which you once walked, following the course of this world, following the prince of the power of the air, the spirit that is now at work in the sons of disobedience." The "spirit of the power of the air" is another name for Satan. All people, therefore, who do not walk with Jesus Christ serve Satan and his demonic co-hort. Satan overpowers the human race, spins his web of lies, and blinds with his deceit. He holds humanity in the grip of eternal slavery, and he has made it his sole occupation to heap misery upon God's creation. Only one can overpower Satan. His name is Jesus of Nazareth, and he is the Son of the living God. He sits enthroned over the cosmos. He defeated the grave and crushed Satan's grip over the universe. Now Jesus endows his people with the message of the gospel—a powerful word that Satan himself cannot overcome.

3. "Receive forgiveness of sins and a place among those who are sanctified by faith." In this final phrase, Jesus proclaims the totality of the gospel promise. Not only will the blind see, not only will Satan's grip crumble, but by faith, people will receive forgiveness of sins and an eternal place in the household of God. The gospel lifts away the weight of sin and ushers the believer into the assurance of salvation secured perfectly through the sacrifice of Christ. The gospel, therefore, lifts the veil that we might see God's beauty, steals us away from the clutches of Satan, and cleanses us of all our sin.

These verses demonstrate Paul's rhetorical skills as he crafts this masterful testimony. On trial for his life, Paul knows that he is not standing before Agrippa by accident. God has sovereignly put him there. God has equipped him and given him the words to speak. Paul homes in on Agrippa and, through the proclamation of his testimony, shoots a gospel arrow into Agrippa. Paul knows that the same gospel that rescued him can transform all who hear it—even a pompous, prideful king.

Questions for reflection

1. Do you have this same conversion story: that is, have you ever repented, asking Jesus to be your Lord and your Savior? If not, would you speak to him now?

2. If you are saved, when was the last time you thanked God for saving someone like you? Do that now!

3. If you had two minutes to explain to someone how your life has been transformed by grace, what would you say?

PART TWO

Acts 26:19-23 contains the heart of Paul's argument as he testifies before Agrippa, Bernice, and Festus. Here, Paul deals with the accusations of the Jews levied against him. The way he dispenses with their accusations is astounding, as he grounds the character of his mission and the message of the gospel in the Old Testament.

Obedience to the Vision and the Message

In **verse 19**, Paul frames his mission not in terms of an elective opportunity or a career path he chose but as a matter of obedience to a heavenly vision. When confronted by the revelation of God, his response constitutes a moral point of decision. Likewise, for us, the Scriptures demand a response. There is no such thing as a neutral answer to God's revelation. We will either respond in obedience or reject God's authority. Paul understood his heavenly vision to come from the throne of God—a decree from the King of kings and Lord of lords. For Paul, therefore, there was no good choice but obedience.

Paul then details the nature of that obedience. He declared his faith to those in Damascus and then progressed throughout the region and then went to the Gentile world (**v 20**). The revelation of God constrained Paul. His fidelity to gospel convictions drove him from region to region, proclaiming the faith he had received on the Damascus road. Specifically, Paul informs his audience that he proclaimed a message of repentance and turning to God—urging his listeners to perform deeds "in keeping with their repentance." Paul packs an enormous depth of theological glory into these few words, which have tremendous bearing for churches today. I want to highlight two particular phrases:

1. "Repent and turn to God." Paul understands the gospel not only as good news but as a summons to repentance. Acceptance of Christ necessarily means turning away from the world and turning toward a life of obedience to God. A host of churches proclaim "gospel messages" devoid of a call to repentance. They

seem to believe that repentance is too harsh a word, pointing to something wrong in a person, something deficient about them. Such negative messages hamper the beauty or attractiveness of the gospel, they fear. They must therefore, they reason, jettison repentance in order to preach more positive feel-good messages.

Without repentance, however, there is no good news. Without turning away from sin, there is no gospel. Preaching which does not proclaim the truth of our condition masquerades a false gospel as good news. Any attempt to cover up the truth of our depravity for fear of offence only endangers humanity even more. Christians must call nonbelievers to repent of their sin. The necessity of repentance points to two things.

First, it points out something wrong in each and every person. The Bible says, "For all have sinned and fallen short of the glory of God," and that "the wages of sin is death" (Romans 3:23; 6:23). Humanity remains under an eternal death sentence. Repentance, therefore, points to a radical depravity inherent in all of us.

Second, however, the truth of our depravity leads to us being able to see the call to repentance as good news. Repentance involves turning away from that which brings death and turning to that which brings life and peace. Repentance breaks the chains which bind us to our sin. The curse of sin, therefore, is not permanent. Change can come. We can repent. God's grace through the sacrifice of his Son secures our ability to repent from our sins, turn to God, and live as new creations in Christ (2 Corinthians 5:21). Repentance is indeed good news.

2. "Performing deeds in keeping with their repentance" (Acts **26:20**). This second phrase balances the two gospel pillars of grace and good works. The Bible clearly teaches salvation by grace alone, through faith alone, in Christ alone. Ephesians 2:8 says, "For by grace you have been saved through faith." Jesus, in John 6:44, said, "No one can come to me unless the Father who sent me draws him." Salvation, therefore, happens through the unmerited

grace of God, who saves his people by his mercy. No one can repent of their own accord. No one can earn their salvation. Only through the gracious and sovereign act of God can anyone come to know him.

Being saved by grace, however, does not permit a lifestyle of rampant, unrepentant sin. Some believe that salvation by grace means a person can disregard the commands and ordinances of God. Paul, however, dispenses with such notions. The Christian faith necessitates a life of repentance—of turning away from sin and pursuing Jesus Christ. Paul makes it clear in Romans 8:12-13: "So then, brothers, we are debtors, not to the flesh, to live according to the flesh. For if you live according to the flesh you will die, but if by the Spirit you put to death the deeds of the body you will live." God summons his people everywhere, in all ages, to a holy life. God says, "You shall be holy to me, for I the Lord am holy and have separated you from the peoples, that you should be mine" (Leviticus 20:26). Grace and works, therefore, unify in a peculiar glory. As the grace of God saves us, the works of repentance naturally flow from our hearts. New creations in Christ live like new creations.

Proclaiming What Moses Predicted

Paul shifts from the powerful telling of his testimony toward the accusations leveled against him. His defense before Agrippa could have begun here. Instead, he leveraged his suffering toward a gospel opportunity and shared the glories of Christ with those lost in the snares of sin. But now it is time to deal with the charges. Acts **26:21-23** reveals the foundation of Paul's message and the absurdity of the charges made against him.

Follow the profound logic of Paul's argument, which shows that the message he proclaimed was really an old message in a new age. First, he says that because he preached the gospel, the Jews tried to kill him (**v 21**). Next, he testifies to God's provision throughout his journeys, which testify to the reality and integrity of his ministry (**v 22**).

Then, Paul announces something astounding. Rather than attributing the foundation of his message to his heavenly vision, or the miracles performed through his hands, or the instruction of Jesus' disciples, Paul specifies that he preached what the prophets had preached. Paul proclaimed exactly what Moses had predicted. In other words, Paul masterfully eviscerates the Jewish charges made against him by grounding the truth of his message in the Hebrew Scriptures. He has only ever proclaimed what was there in the text of the Old Testament. He preached what God had revealed long ago, in ages past.

What did God reveal in ages past through the prophets and through Moses? Paul says that it was "that the Christ must suffer and that, by being the first to rise from the dead, he would proclaim light both to our people and to the Gentiles" (**v 23**). He reveals that God's redemptive plan spanned all the ages. Genesis, Exodus, Leviticus, Numbers, Deuteronomy, and the entire Old Testament pointed to the coming of God's suffering Messiah, who would not only suffer but die; and not only die but be raised from the grave. The clearest expression of God's plan, implemented through the suffering of his Son, comes from Isaiah 53:3-6. The prophet writes:

"He was despised and rejected by men, a man of sorrows and acquainted with grief; and as one from whom men hide their faces he was despised, and we esteemed him not. Surely he has borne our griefs and carried our sorrows; yet we esteemed him stricken, smitten by God, and afflicted. But he was pierced for our transgressions; he was crushed for our iniquities; upon him was the chastisement that brought us peace, and with his wounds we are healed. All we like sheep have gone astray; we have turned—every one—to his own way; and the Lord has laid on him the iniquity of us all."

Jesus fulfilled this prophecy in full. He became the man of sorrows and took on our grief. God smote Jesus and laid upon him the fullness of his wrath for our sin. The nails which pierced Jesus' flesh fulfilled Isaiah 53. The Father's crushing of the Son had been revealed there in the book of Isaiah. God did not accidentally sacrifice his Son, nor was the cross "Plan B." God willed the death of his Son for our sins from the dawning of creation and whispered the news of Jesus' future sacrifice through the ministry of the prophets. Here, in Acts 26, Paul pronounces his identity as a herald of that very message. Now, though, it is no longer whispered. Jesus has come and fulfilled the prophetic witness. Signs and whispers have given way to the thundering glory of Jesus' death and resurrection from the grave.

Paul, therefore, stands before King Agrippa and the Roman authorities and proclaims the excellences of the gospel as prophesied in ages past. The apostle grounds his authority in nothing less than the revelation of the God of the universe. The Jews cannot stop him. The Romans shall not silence him. Paul has a message from the throne of God which he must announce. As Christians today, we need the same sense of urgency and mission found in the apostle. The church declares a message not of its own crafting, but a proclamation from the heavenly throneroom. The importance of a message's content derives from the source of the message. The source of the gospel is God himself. He has commissioned his people to serve as his ambassadors and to proclaim that truth, whatever the cost. Paul, in Acts 26, heralds the good news of the gospel, even with his life on the line.

Why We Preach the Gospel

The moment Paul mentions Jesus' resurrection, Festus, the Roman governor, interrupts Paul's speech and charges him with lunacy, and says that his "great learning" is driving him out of his mind (Acts **26:24**). Interestingly, when Paul addressed the Areopagus in chapter 17, the Athenians mocked his ignorance. Now, however, Festus believes Paul is too educated. The determination to reject the gospel will reach for any straw.

The Christian gospel, however, is not irrational. Paul even says his words flow from truth and rationality (**26:25**). On the other hand, the gospel is not rationalistic. None come to understand the gospel through an intellectual exercise or superior powers of reason. We do not figure out the gospel through our own ingenuity. The gospel is rational, but minds darkened by sin cannot grasp its truthfulness except through God's grace and mercy.

Paul rejects this charge of insanity and makes a final appeal to King Agrippa. His appeal, however, aims not at his release. He knows he has appealed to Caesar and will make his case before the emperor. Paul, therefore, makes a final appeal for Agrippa to repent and believe in the gospel. Paul points out the king's knowledge of his ministry and then says, "King Agrippa, do you believe the prophets? I know that you believe" (**v 26-27**). Paul dramatically shifts the entire scene. The hearing began with Paul on trial. Now, however, Agrippa is under interrogation. Paul confronts Agrippa with a piercing question laced with a summons to repent and believe in the gospel.

The narrative immediately moves to Agrippa's answer. The king does not reject the premise of Paul's message; he only points out the brevity of his exposure to the gospel (**v 28**). Instead, he attempts to move the focus of the hearing back to Paul through his questioning of Paul's attempt to convert him, to which Paul retorts, "I would to God that not only you but also all who hear me this day might become such as I am—except for these chains" (**v 29**). So Paul ends with an appeal to the entire audience. This is incredible! Paul, a prisoner in chains, says (in effect) to the king in his royal robes and the crowds of cultural elites, *However high you climb and whatever wealth you enjoy, you do not have what I have found. You ache for what I possess, and you need it far more than you realize.* Paul does not let the success of the king or the governor, or all those around him adorned in their wealth and power, deter him from his mission. He sees right through their pomp and prosperity. The eternal riches of Christ eclipse all the wealth and power this world can offer.

This is why we preach the gospel. We preach that others might taste and see that the Lord is good. We proclaim the good news that others might enjoy the splendor and majesty of Christ. We enjoin our neighbors, our families, and our coworkers to come and know Christ because we have come to understand the glory of his forgiveness, the beauty of his grace, and the riches of joy in his being. We want them to enjoy all that we enjoy in the gospel. How can we keep it to ourselves?

The king's response to Paul reminds us that in our evangelism we may not always or ever see a **revival** break out when we proclaim God's word. Evangelism takes time. Christians cast out gospel seeds. God gives the growth. God has called us to faithfulness; and he will tend to the rest. Yes, we present our messages persuasively. Yes, we urge our hearers to repent. It is God, however, who completes the work. You and I, like the apostle Paul, must simply be faithful to proclaim.

The chapter ends with the authorities conferring with one another recognizing Paul's innocence (**v 30-32**). Indeed, Paul could have been released from his chains if he had not appealed to Caesar. But since he had, Festus had no choice but to send Paul to Rome. Again, make no mistake: that is exactly what Paul wanted because that is precisely what God intended. Even in the hands of unbelieving authorities, Paul remained in the constant, perfect providential care of his loving Father, who would continue to use Paul in Rome for glorious purposes.

Questions for reflection

1. Is your general view of repentance something that you have to do, or something that God kindly gives you to lead you closer to him? What difference do those two views make to someone's Christian life?

2. Is there a way you need to start, or re-start, performing deeds in keeping with your profession of repentance and faith?

3. "Evangelism takes time. Christians cast out gospel seeds." How does this view of witnessing keep us both patient and persistent?

12. GOD'S KINGDOM AT THE EMPIRE'S HEART

Acts 27 ushers in a climactic demonstration of God's providence and sovereignty. Throughout this chapter and the next, Paul faces very arduous situations. Yet, as the narrative unfolds, readers quite clearly see that Paul is right where God wants him. Thus, Acts 27 presents a picture of God's hand providentially orchestrating human decisions and natural events to accomplish his perfect will.

An Ominous Voyage

Paul, who is now a political prisoner, embarks on a long and demanding journey across the Mediterranean Sea (**v 3**). Julius, a centurion of the Augustan **Cohort**, escorts him on the journey to Rome (**v 1**). The Augustan Cohort, also known as the Imperial Cohort, had direct responsibility for protecting Caesar. Julius, however, is not Paul's only travel companion: Luke includes himself as a fellow-traveler (**v 2**). Aristarchus is also mentioned. As Paul's friend, Aristarchus served Paul by voluntarily traveling with him. Yet Aristarchus' presence suggests something ominous. The Jews feared the sea, possibly due to the Old Testament accounts of Noah and Jonah. Paul's nerves were therefore likely on edge for the voyage at sea; perhaps Aristarchus came along for comfort.

The journey's timing also speaks to its ominous nature. The best seasons for navigating the Mediterranean are the spring and summer.

But **verse 9** reveals that this trip took place after "the fast"—the **Day of Atonement**, or Yom Kippur—had ended, in mid-October. This trip, therefore, took place in the autumn and presented a grave threat to the travelers' safety. This threat shows itself as early as **verse 4**, when Luke describes the winds as "against us," forcing the ship to divert.

Despite the detour, the ship makes relatively good time (**v 5**). But Julius doesn't think they are going fast enough. Often mistakes occur when one perceives progress as trudging along too slowly. If Julius had been willing to stay on the Adramyttian ship and go from coastal city to coastal city, they likely would have arrived in Italy and been able to go up the Via Appia toward Rome long before they actually did. Instead, Julius chose to board a much larger Alexandrian ship (**v 6**).

Adramyttian ships were typically sixty feet (18m) long, and rough seawaters could easily swamp them. Alexandrian ships were roughly 180 feet (55m) in length, forty-eight feet (14.5m) wide, and forty feet (12m) high. They were the largest ships produced at the time. Though larger, these ships came with their own host of problems and dangers. Not only was this particular ship carrying 276 people (**v 37**), but these ships also customarily carried grain in their holds. These holds ran the length and width of the ship and were six feet (2m) deep. When filled with grain, the ship took on enormous weight. Further, this grain would be shifted in the holds by the action of the waves, causing a rocking effect that made stabilization challenging for the ship's captain.

Even more danger arose if the hold took on water. When grain gets wet, it expands and gains weight. If a ship sprung a leak, it would gradually sink—but before it went under the waves, the wet grain would expand and literally break apart the ship. Once a leak started, it was too late to save the grain, which soaks up water very quickly. So this was yet another element of danger affecting this trip, and **verses 7-8** make it clear that the ship proceeded with difficulty. One final significant thing to mention is that any captain who could deliver grain to Rome in winter was paid a premium. So the captain of this Alexandrian ship must have been very ambitious, which explains much of the following account.

Desperation Mode

In **verse 8**, the travelers arrive in Fair Havens. This coastal city earned its name because of its calm weather during most of the year. Our travelers, however, make port at the wrong time of year. During the winter, the water got very shallow. If a storm occurred, ships in the shallows could run aground and be destroyed. It makes sense, then, that the captain of the Alexandrian ship does not want to stay there long. Paul, however, gives his own nautical advice, urging the centurion to not press on in the journey (**v 9-10**). According to **verse 11**, he is heard but not followed. This matters because the crew will affirm Paul's credibility later on.

Since Fair Havens is an unsuitable winter harbor, the captain decides to set sail toward the double-harbor city of Phoenix, a fifteen mile journey (**v 12-13**). Phoenix had one port facing north and another facing south. This made it perfect for winter harboring because depending on the wind direction, the peninsula offered protection on at least one side. The trip to Phoenix, however, proves disastrous. The ship has to traverse a small yet treacherous stretch of sea that offers no protection from the Mediterranean winds. As they sail, a great northeaster wind blows down from Crete. Rather than allowing them to sail close to Crete, this rushing wind causes them to lose control of the ship (**v 14-15**). Instead of docking for the winter at Phoenix, the ship is pushed by the wind out into the open sea. This is bad news for the sailors.

The next verses continue to give further glimpses of the sailors' despair. Ancient ships would tow a lifeboat behind the main vessel, but during storms the lifeboat could ram the ship and punch a hole in it. This presented a major issue, particularly as it endangered all of the grain in the holds. To avoid this disaster, the lifeboat is raised (**v 16**). Then the sailors begin frapping the ship (**v 17**)—that is, wrapping the vessel with ropes and cables in an effort to hold it together. Frapping could help, but it would not save a ship from sinking; it would only buy some time. Frapping was only resorted to in extreme desperation. Then, for further precaution, they begin throwing the cargo overboard (**v 18**). They have to lighten the ship because they are afraid of water getting into the hold and expanding the grain. To avoid sinking, the crew dump their own source of income—the main reason for which they had set sail.

Things only get worse. After losing their cargo, the crew are forced to throw out the ship's tackle (**v 19**). The tackle was used in hoisting and lowering the sails; its loss left the ship without means of navigation or propulsion. It was the ultimate act of desperation. At this point, therefore, the crew are simply giving themselves to the storm in the hopes of riding it out or being rescued. Their hope, however, quickly fades away over the horizon (**v 20**). Even Luke loses hope—clearly he does not possess the confident faith of Paul. Paul knows God will get him and the company to Rome. 23:11 continues to drive the narrative. Paul lived as he did because he kept his mind set on the promises of God. Paul, therefore, steps in to offer much needed encouragement.

Confidence in God's Sovereignty

Paul stands up in **27:21** and begins with an "I told you so!" This may seem as if Paul intends to chide the wayward travelers. In fact, he attempts to assert his credibility as a voice of reason. In **verse 22**, he enjoins the passengers not to give up but to take heart. He promises, "There will be no loss of life among you, but only of the ship." Paul then reveals the origin of his knowledge: an angel of God has instructed him to have no fear because God has willed that Paul should testify before Caesar. The angel has also promised Paul the safety of every soul on board the ship (**v 23-24**). Paul concludes by stating, "So take heart, men, for I have faith in God that it will be exactly as I have been told" (**v 25**).

Paul's words provide three vital applications. First, he exudes an unyielding confidence in God's sovereign will. Time and again, Paul refuses to allow his circumstances to dictate his theology. When presented with trials, difficulties, and persecution, Paul rests in God's perfect will. He trusts his God and presses on in faithfulness, whatever the cost. Christians today might jettison our hope in God's will, even when we only find ourselves stuck in heavy traffic, making us late for an appointment. Paul, conversely, maintains his confidence in God when shipwreck looks certain. It is Paul's convictions about God that enables his continued faithfulness and empowers his encouraging word to the other sailors.

Second, Paul remains confident in the Lord, even when his circumstances seem unnecessary. If God intended Paul to testify to the gospel before Caesar, why then did Paul have to endure more trials and more difficulty? God could have willed that Paul would make it to Rome speedily. Instead, God takes Paul to Rome on the seas of struggle. The difficult journey, however, leads Paul into a greater dependence upon God. Moreover, Paul will provide a faithful witness to all those on board of the goodness and sovereign power of the one true God. Acts 27 reveals that our road might be longer and harder than we imagined. Indeed, we might even question the will of God and why he has brought us on such a perilous journey. But we can, and must, trust in God. His will is perfect, and he calls us to rest in his plans.

Finally, in **27:26**, Paul says, "But we must run aground on some island." Though Paul rests in God's sovereign hand, he knows that humans bear a responsibility to act in accordance with God's will. God summons us to faith and obedience. These two virtues of the Christian life mark two sides of the same coin. While we must trust in God's will and his sovereign purposes, our trust evidences itself through acts of obedience. In the Exodus story, Israel not only needed to believe that God would pass over their houses; they also had to sacrifice a lamb and paint its blood on their doorposts. In Acts 27, Paul calls the ship's crew and passengers to faith in God, while also directing them to run the ship aground as an act of faith.

Paul no longer speaks like a prisoner. He is in the custody of the Roman justice system, yes, but **verse 24** informs us that God has given all the travelers into Paul's hands. The apostle's imprisonment, therefore, does not imprison God's sovereignty nor does it shackle the power of the gospel. Indeed, the most powerful man on the ship is not the captain or the centurion. Paul, the prisoner of Rome, possesses power because he is a prisoner of the Lord Jesus Christ, who has endowed Paul with God's revelation.

> The apostle's imprisonment does not shackle the power of the gospel.

Verses 27-32 chronicle an episode which displays Paul's authority over the vessel and the trust the sailors placed in Paul. The wayward sailors, their sight obscured by darkness, believe their ship is approaching a shoreline. Naturally, they begin to lower the lifeboat (**v 28-29**). Paul, however, warns that any who venture into the lifeboat will lose their life. Paul does not offer sound nautical counsel because the issue here is not one of nautical science but theology. Paul continues to direct the crew through the revelation of God.

Verses 33-36 give us another glimpse of Paul's calm trust in the providence of God. As the uncontrollable ship is blown toward certain shipwreck, Paul advises the crew to sit, rest, and take a meal. It has been 14 days since they ate, and they abide by Paul's instruction. As they all sit down to eat, Paul gives thanks to God. His prayer to and praise of God exemplify trust, serenity, and gratitude toward God. Paul's demeanor before the crew, no doubt, had a profound impact and gospel witness.

After their meal, the crew get back to the work of jettisoning weight to make the inevitable shipwreck less severe (**v 37-40**). But when the ship strikes a reef in open water, the front of the vessel is jammed, while the back of the boat continues to be assaulted by the sea (**v 41**). Naturally, the boat begins to break apart. The soldiers know that if they go back to Rome without their prisoners, having let them escape, they will face the same judgment as the prisoners would have done. So they devise a plan to kill the prisoners and blame it on the extreme situation (**v 42**). The centurion, however, thwarts the mass murder as he has developed a trust in Paul (**v 43**). The centurion orders everyone who can to jump overboard and swim for dry land. Those who cannot swim grab hold of planks from the ship and float to safety (**v 44**). The whole chapter, right up to the very last verse, presents us with a remarkable picture of God's sovereignty and power. Nothing will thwart the will of God.

Indeed, nothing will stop God's will or hinder his purposes for his church. In this age, God does not promise his people a life free from suffering and trials. Paul endured much for the cause of the gospel. But he pressed on because of God's promise. Christians today sometimes fail in zealous obedience because we lose sight of the spectacular reward that awaits those who obey God. God has promised an eternity unlike anything we can imagine. He has promised that we will be with him, face to face—that death will be no more and sin will pass away. There will be no more tears. No more death. No more sadness. No more grief. God calls his people to seize his promises and hold them tight. Our obedience will only be as strong as our faith in the promises of God. Paul said in **verse 25**, "So take heart ... for I have faith in God that it will be exactly as I have been told." Does the church today possess such faith? Do we believe in the promises of God? Do we live as if we believe in his promises?

Questions for reflection

1. Think of situations and circumstances in your life in which you clearly saw (or can now see, looking back) the Lord's providence. How can the reality of God's providence change the way you handle present or future trials in your life?

2. What (if anything) holds you back from having the same confidence in the Lord that Paul expresses in verses 22-25? Are you praying for that kind of calm trust?

3. What will it mean for your life today to live truly believing that God's promises are true?

PART TWO

In Acts 27, Paul and the naval crew survived the shipwreck because of God's sovereign plan. The final chapter of Acts concludes on a similar note of God's providential care for his apostle and the spread of the gospel. Chapter 28 serves as the climatic end to this account of God's work in the early church and its great expansion, and leaves us looking forward, recognizing that God is still moving in and through his church, which is exactly what the rest of the New Testament and all of church history proclaim.

The Miracles on Malta

Everyone on the Alexandrian ship made it safely through the shipwreck and onto the island of Malta (**28:1**). Once on land, the travelers encountered inhabitants who showed all those on the ship extraordinary kindness, providing them with means of comfort and hospitality (**v 2**). Yet the narrative almost instantly confronts us with another remarkably unfortunate event in Paul's life. While he is moving some sticks onto the fire, a venomous snake strikes the apostle (**v 3**). In a day when there was no anti-venom, this bite would certainly have been expected to lead to a tragic death for Paul.

The islanders believed that this was an act of cosmic justice (**v 4**). In the pagan worldview, the universe had judged Paul and struck him through the fangs of a venomous snake. This "cause-and-effect" worldview still exists in much of the world today, and is found in notions like *karma*—do something wrong in this universe, and the universe will repay you. In Maltese thinking, therefore, a snake bit Paul because he had sinned. Christians must not draw hasty conclusions like this, for they stem from a pagan worldview and understanding of events. Paul, unlike the islanders, trusted in the providence of God and maintained his composure. He shook off the snake as though nothing had happened (**v 5**). Everyone believed Paul would soon die. The worldview governing the pagans, however, would soon succumb to the prevailing, powerful, and sovereign glory of the true God. Indeed, Paul did not die—and so the islanders concluded that Paul was actually a god (**v 6**).

Verses 7-10 show the continuing generosity of the inhabitants; this was perhaps heightened by their belief that Paul was divine. The richest citizen of Malta, Publius, personally cared for the entire sea-faring group for three days. After he had finished entertaining the visitors, it seems that the rest of the island's citizens pitched in to care for the nearly 300 tired and hungry guests for the next three months (**v 11**). The narrative also shows how Paul helped many on the island. In **verse 8**, Paul heals the father of Publius, and then the entire island comes to Paul to have illnesses and diseases cured (**v 8-9**). Luke does not provide much information about the miracles at Malta. In other passages where crowds believed Paul to be a god, Luke tells us exactly how Paul handled the situation and stewarded such opportunities toward declaring the gospel. Here, however, Luke includes no such details. We can, however, deduce that God used these events and worked through them to his glory. Paul would not have performed any miracles except by the power of God working in and through him. If at any point Paul had begun to dignify the islanders' belief in his divinity, God would surely have removed his hand from Paul and his ministry. The presence of God with Paul on Malta, therefore, points to the gospel and the power of God at work among the inhabitants of Malta and the shipwrecked crew.

To Rome

After waiting in Malta from November through January—months when cold and dangerous winds would come from the north—the voyagers set sail again (**v 11**). They were able to enjoy southerly winds coming from the Sahara Desert in North Africa, which would have eliminated the threat of dangerous thunderstorms. The gentle breezes of the Mediterranean would now serve them, rather than assault them, and lead their vessel toward its final destination. They boarded another Alexandrian ship, which had the Greek gods Castor and Pollux as a figurehead.

In Greek mythology these twin brothers were semidivine sons of Leda. They may have appeared on the front of the ship as a nod to the pagan gods, or possibly to act as a brand marker that identified the ship with a particular shipping line. Whatever the case, this was the ship that Paul and Luke had to take.

Their first stop was the big natural harbor of Syracuse, on the island of Sicily (**v 12**). After staying there three days, they sailed around to Rhegium and then on to Puteoli, known today as Pozzuoli (**v 13**). This is a harbor in Naples, Italy. To get from Syracuse to Puteoli, a ship had to traverse a very narrow strait about two miles wide between the islands of Sicily and Italy. Whirlpools were one of the natural dangers to mariners traveling through. Nevertheless, the route was convenient because ships would otherwise have had to travel all the way around Sicily to the west, and the winds would have been very unfriendly when making a turn back to the east. And so they arrived, and found Christians at Puteoli (**v 14**).

How had Christianity made it to Puteoli? Here is a reminder that the advancement of the gospel did not rest upon the shoulders of Paul alone. The hero of Acts is not Paul or Peter. It is God himself, who powerfully advanced the gospel through-

> God has more zeal for kingdom work than the greatest missionaries in history.

out the known world. God has more zeal for kingdom work than any of the greatest missionaries in Christian history. The mission of the gospel rises above any one individual. God did not need Paul. He does not need you. He does, however, summon all his people to join in the mission of salvation. Christians, by God's grace, have the glorious opportunity to join God in his kingdom work and be used by him as his ambassadors.

So, in **verse 15**, Paul finally arrives in Rome. Word of Paul's arrival had spread to the various Christian communities in the region.

Many came from far and wide to greet Paul and encourage him in the task that lay before him. Indeed, Luke writes, "On seeing them, Paul thanked God and took courage." Even the apostle Paul needed encouragement. Today's Christian culture venerates "Christian celebrities." Some Christian communities tend to put their leaders on a pedestal. Those leaders, however, perched on their pillars of praise, might have few, if any, brothers and sisters in the faith encouraging them and holding them accountable for their walk with God. Christian leaders need, in an urgent and profound way, the encouragement and love of those whom they serve. So it was here. Paul faced an enormous trial. He soon would have a face-to-face meeting with the most powerful man in the world—the emperor of Rome. Paul needed help, and he found strength in the company and care of God's people. Those who serve as ministry leaders must learn from Paul's example. He needed the help of those he served. Seek out the refreshment of biblical fellowship and ensure your own life remains accountable to other brothers and sisters in the faith. For those who enjoy the leadership of particular Christian men and women, encourage them without idolizing them or flattering them. Like Paul, these leaders may face significant challenges. A word of encouragement can go a long way in helping them press on in faithful obedience.

Still Witnessing

Verse 17 presents us with a very unusual situation. When Paul arrived in Rome and was placed under solitary house arrest (**v 16**), we might have expected him to go get a good attorney. After all, he was brought there to be tried for his life. But of course, throughout Paul's ministry, the first place he went to in new cities was the synagogue. Paul could not go to the synagogue in Rome, though, because he remained under house arrest. Paul, therefore, did the next best thing: he called the Jewish leaders to his house. He brought the synagogue to himself (**v 17**).

Having done this, Paul summarizes the reason why he has come to Rome as a prisoner (**v 17b-19**). He recounts the events in Jerusalem, professes his innocence, and then says something astounding to the Jewish elders: "For this reason, therefore, I have asked to see you and speak with you, since it is because of the hope of Israel that I am wearing this chain" (**v 20**). Paul declares his allegiance to the people of Israel and the heritage of his nation: indeed, he boldly states that he possesses the hope of Israel through the message he has received. Paul says his hope has led to his chains.

Word about Paul's accusations from Jerusalem had not reached Rome before he did (**v 21**). Still, the Jews wanted him to give an account of his message because it was being spoken against everywhere (**v 22**). Here we see the conflict was not only between the church and Judaism but also between the church and Rome. In other words, wherever Christianity went, it upset everything in that region. Christianity was—and still is today—a disruptive force for those set against it.

Of course, Paul was obliged to proclaim his message everywhere, so at the appointed time, he spent all day testifying to the truth of the gospel and the fulfillment of the prophetic witness in Jesus Christ. Both in **verse 23** and later in **verse 31**, we read that Paul preached about the kingdom of God. This was not the customary way for Paul to describe the gospel, but here (and earlier, in chapter 20) he speaks about the kingdom of God and the gospel of the God's grace as being the same reality. Notice, too, that he does this by preaching Christ from the Old Testament Scriptures. The Jews heard his message and were divided over it—some believed and some did not (**v 24**). But after they had listened all day, Paul began to lose his audience.

At this point, Paul proclaimed to the Jews a prophetic word from Isaiah. He quotes from Isaiah 6:9-10, where God spoke to Isaiah to indicate that even after the prophet had preached, the people would not listen. God told Isaiah at the start of his mission that his preaching would have no effect on the people of Israel. The people had hardened their hearts, shut their eyes, and turned away from God. In quoting from Isaiah 6 to these Jews in Rome, Paul applies this prophetic judgment to them. In choosing not to heed Paul's words, they reveal their true character as those in a long line of hardened sinners who have rejected the promise of salvation secured through the Messiah. The mentioning of the Holy Spirit in Acts **28:25** grounds the authority of Paul's pronouncement not in Paul but in God himself. God has judged the Jews in Paul's audience because they have turned from his gospel. In other words, when God promised Isaiah that Israel would reject his message, he not only spoke of the people in Isaiah's day but of all who fail to repent and believe.

During Paul's day, Rome had ten synagogues that hosted about forty thousand Jews, but most of the Christians in Rome were Gentiles. That was a sign of the future of the church. Indeed, Luke has recorded throughout the book of Acts that the gospel will meet a positive response in the most surprising of places and from the most unlikely of people. The gospel saved an Ethiopian eunuch. Paul himself could not resist the grace of the gospel. A Gentile Roman centurion received Christ. Lydia, a businesswoman, became a slave of Christ. A slave girl was freed by Christ. A Philippian jailer melted before God of the universe. The gospel moves in surprising ways and draws in people from the most unlikely of backgrounds.

> The gospel will meet a positive response in the most surprising of places and from the most unlikely of people.

At this word from Isaiah, the Jews left him, still disputing with each other—an argument that continues to this day (**v 29**—though not all the earliest manuscripts include this verse). After that, Paul continued living in Rome and preaching the gospel for two years (**v 30-31**). In essence, God had Paul, in Rome, doing exactly what he wanted. The shackles of man would not hinder Paul. Though he was a man in chains, he preached a Savior who would set the captive free. Though he was a man in bondage, he never stopped preaching Christ.

The Next Chapter

Some say the book of Acts is a biography of the apostles Peter and Paul. But this is far too limited a view. Rather, Acts contains a beautiful biography of the early church and its faithfulness in spreading the gospel to the ends of the earth. Moreover, Acts chronicles a faithful God who keeps his promises, preserves his church, advances his message, and establishes an eternal people.

Luke's conclusion of Acts brings the book to a climactic end, leaving us exactly where the Holy Spirit wants us—ready for the next chapter. That chapter continues to be written today. The gospel still advances to the ends of the earth, and God has called all his people to live as protagonists in this glorious chapter. Luke ends his narrative with an implied question: Peter preached the kingdom in Jerusalem; Philip proclaimed Christ in Samaria; Paul announced Christ around the Roman Empire. Where will *you* go? Will the church today fail in its divine mandate, or will we, like the apostle Paul, march forward in faith, with zeal for God, and hold on to his promises? We face a task unfinished—may God grant us the strength and courage to stand in that long line of Spirit-empowered, faithful witnesses which stretches all the way back to that unlikely band of first-century pioneers—those men and women who, filled with God's Spirit, did indeed turn the world upside down.

Questions for reflection

1. In what ways can the church today be too quick to draw conclusions about someone's sin when they suffer, and someone's integrity or calling when they succeed?

2. The book of Acts has taken us from a few dozen believers in a single city to a multitude of churches throughout the Mediterranean—all in one generation. How does this excite you about your gospel witness today?

3. In what way(s) has the Holy Spirit been changing you through reading Acts 13 – 28?

GLOSSARY

Aphrodite: Greek goddess of love.

Apologist: someone who defends something with reasoned arguments.

Apollo: Greek god of the sun.

Apollos: early Christian leader who preached in Ephesus and Corinth.

Apostle: one of those appointed directly by the risen Christ to teach about him with authority.

Atoning: providing a way of coming back into friendship with someone.

Baptize: to sprinkle with or immerse in water, in a public ceremony which signifies the welcoming of someone into the church as a member of God's people, through faith in Jesus Christ.

Biblical ethic: the way Christians ought to behave, according to the Bible.

Blasphemous: when God is disrespected or mocked.

Caucasians: people of European ethnic origin.

Cheap grace: a distortion of the gospel which leaves out the need for us to confess and change.

Christ: God's anointed or chosen one. In the Old Testament, God promised that the Christ would come to rescue and rule his people. The Hebrew word for "Christ" is "Messiah."

Christendom: the area of the world where a form of Christianity is either the state religion or dominates the culture and is subscribed to by the majority of citizens.

Christology: the study of who Christ is: particularly his nature as both human and divine, and the way in which he saves his people.

Circumcision: the ceremony undergone by Jewish boys in which the foreskin is cut off. God told the men among his people in the Old Testament to be circumcised as a way to show physically that they knew and trusted him, and belonged to the people of God (see Genesis 17).

Claudius: the fourth emperor of Rome, who ruled from AD 41 to 54.

Cohort: a Roman military unit of somewhere between 300 and 800 soldiers.

Consecration: appointing someone to fulfill a particular role or task for God.

Conversion: the moment when someone for the first time recognizes Jesus, God's Son, as Lord, and turns to him as Savior.

Conviction: convincing a person that something is true.

Cornelius: a Roman Gentile centurion who became a Christian (Acts 10).

David: the second king of Israel, whose reign was the high point of Israel's history. He was also the writer of many psalms. God promised that one of David's descendants would reign forever—the Messiah (see 2 Samuel 7).

Day of Atonement: a Jewish holy day in which specific sacrifices were made, recognizing human sin and asking God to forgive it (see Leviticus 16). This is still observed every year by Jews.

Deacons: literally table-waiters; in the church, deacons are church members appointed to serve the church in practical ways.

Deeds of the body: sin. In Romans 8, Paul contrasts the body, which represents our natural state of sinfulness leading to death, with the Holy Spirit, which represents the eternal life given to us in Christ.

Denomination: a branch of the Christian church, such as Pentecostalism or Lutheranism.

Doctrine: a set of beliefs or principles which are taught as part of a religion.

Ecumenical council: a gathering of the leaders of the worldwide church, to agree and clarify what Christians should do or believe about a particular point. There were a series of these councils in the centuries after Christianity became the official religion of the Roman Empire.

Dogma: a fixed set of beliefs or principles.

Elders: the leaders of a local church, responsible for its teaching and ministry.

Evangelist: one who shares the good news about Jesus Christ with non-Christians.

Evangelistic: sharing the good news about Jesus Christ.

Exclusivist: shutting out particular people or groups.

Exorcism: casting out an evil spirit from a person who appears to be possessed. This was done by Jesus numerous times in the Gospel accounts, and later by others who prayed in the name of Jesus.

Epistle: a New Testament letter to a church (or churches) or a person.

Hyperbole: exaggeration.

Fall: the moment when Eve and Adam disobeyed God and ate from the tree of the knowledge of good and evil (see Genesis 3). From this moment onwards, all humans have been naturally sinful.

Free city: a city that governs itself rather than submitting to a higher ruler. Some cities under the Roman Empire were given this status.

Gentile: people who are not ethnically Jewish.

Hades: the Greek and Roman god of the underworld, or the name given to the underworld itself.

Heresy: false teaching that, if believed, causes someone to reject the gospel in some way.

Incarnated: having become human.

Inerrancy: when something contains no mistakes or untruths.

Inspired: given words or understanding by God. The authors of the New Testament were inspired by God as they wrote.

Isthmus: a narrow strip of land with water on either side.

Judea: the region around Jerusalem.

Kingdom work: proclaiming the gospel, with the aim that people will turn to Jesus and put their lives under his rule.

Laying hands on: placing a hand on someone as a sign of prayer.

Levitical: coming from the book of Leviticus, which contains many of the commands which God gave to Moses.

Lost (the): those who do not accept Jesus as Lord, and therefore will not enjoy eternal life with him.

Messiah: see **Christ**.

Metaphor: an image which is used to explain something, but is not to be taken literally (e.g. "The news was a dagger to his heart").

Militant atheist: someone who does not believe that God exists, and aggressively tries to persuade others of this.

Missiological: relating to the way in which mission is carried out and the good news about Jesus is shared.

Mosaic laws: the commands given by God to his people through Moses. These set out how believers in the Old Testament should relate to God and to one another. They are written down in the books of Exodus, Leviticus, Numbers and Deuteronomy.

Moses: the leader of God's people at the time when God brought them out of slavery in Egypt.

Nazarene: someone from Nazareth. Early Christians were known as "Nazarenes" because Jesus was from Nazareth.

New covenant: a covenant is a binding agreement or promise. The old covenant set out how believers in the Old Testament related to God; Jesus established the new covenant, so believers now relate to God through Jesus' saving death and resurrection.

Nirvana: a state of freedom from suffering which Buddhists believe can be achieved by removing all sense of self.

Occult: practices which involve or appeal to supernatural powers other than God.

Old covenant: a covenant is a binding agreement or promise. The old covenant set out how believers in the Old Testament could relate to God. Christians now relate to God through Jesus in the new covenant.

Omnipotent: all-powerful.

Oratory: the art of giving public speeches.

Orthodoxy: standard, accepted Christian teaching.

Oxymoron: something made up of elements or words which seem to contradict each other (e.g. "cruel kindness")

Pagan: a word used in the Bible to refer to non-Christians (e.g. 1 Peter 2:12; 4:3-5). Pagan religion (generally speaking) refers to a traditional belief system that includes many gods who are unpredictable, and whose favor or blessing or protection needs to be bought or earned through ritual or sacrifice.

Paradigm: a template or pattern to be followed.

Passover: Jewish festival which commemorated the time when God rescued his people from slavery in Egypt. He did this by sending plagues, the last of which was the death of each family's firstborn. This could be avoided only by killing a lamb in the firstborn's place, so that God's judgment would "pass over" that household (see Exodus 12 – 13).

Pentecost: when God gave his Holy Spirit to the believers after Jesus had ascended to heaven. See Acts 2:1-41.

Pharisee: a member of a first-century Jewish sect which was extremely strict about keeping God's laws, and added extra laws around God's law to ensure that it wouldn't be broken.

Pluralistic: with regard to religion, the view that all religious viewpoints are equally valid and none are exclusively true in any way.

Postmodernism: a movement in Western culture which began in the mid-20th century. Postmodernist thinkers tend to say that there is no single truth or system that applies to everything. Instead they emphasize the idea that anyone's perspective can be true for them.

Praetorium: Roman governor's headquarters.

Proconsul: a high-ranking Roman official.

Procurator: governor of a Roman province.

Profession of faith: declaring that you believe in Jesus Christ and have accepted him as Savior.

Prophesy: to speak words from God, given by the Holy Spirit.

Proselytizing: when someone tries to persuade others to believe the same things as them.

Prosperity gospel: the false teaching that God rewards faith with good health or greater wealth, and that Christians should expect and seek these things.

Providential: the truth that God is overseeing all events.

Redemptive history: the process throughout history by which God has rescued and will rescue his people from sin to live with him forever.

Redemption: being saved from sin; being bought back or regained by God. In Paul's time, one could redeem and so free a slave by paying their owner. By dying on the cross, Jesus paid the full price for sin.

Revival: when a large number of people come to faith at the same time.

Rhetoric: the art of giving public speeches, particularly in order to persuade an audience.

Roman citizen: someone in the Roman Empire who had the right to the vote and to a fair trial, and who was protected by law from being tortured. This was a special status which not everyone who lived under the Roman Empire enjoyed.

Sabbath: the weekly day of rest and worship which God commanded for his people.

Sacraments: certain ceremonies which Roman Catholics believe must be performed in order to gain salvation. Protestants also use the word "sacraments" with regard to baptism and the Lord's Supper, but do not view them as necessary acts for someone to be saved.

Saints: Christians.

Salvific: leading to salvation.

Sanctification: the process by which, with the help of the Holy Spirit, Christians become holier; that is, more like Christ.

Sanhedrin: the Jewish ruling council and law court.

Sect: small religious group that has separated from the main religion.

Sedition: speaking or acting in a way that encourages people to rebel against the government.

Shema: Moses' declaration of the nature of God in Deuteronomy 6:4: "Hear, O Israel: The Lord our God, the Lord is one." This phrase is used as a prayer in Judaism.

Sovereign: royal; all-powerful.

Stephen: the first Christian to be killed for his faith (see Acts 7).

Steward: to use or manage circumstances or possessions for a particular purpose.

Stumbling block: an obstacle to belief in Christ.

Syncretism: the mixing of beliefs from different religions or traditions.

Theological: focusing on God's perspective and the truth about him.

Torah: the first five books of the Bible, which contain the law of God revealed to Moses.

Transgressions: sins or wrongdoing.

Tree: here, meaning the cross of Jesus.

Western Text: there are thousands of manuscripts, or handwritten copies, of different parts of the Bible, dating from the first century onwards. These are divided into "families." The Western Text is one such family: a group of manuscripts of the Greek New Testament, thought to have been produced mainly in the Western Roman Empire.

Worldview: the beliefs we hold in an attempt to make sense of the world as we experience it, and which direct how we live in it. Everyone has a worldview.

Yahweh: the name by which God revealed himself to Moses (Exodus 3:13-14). Literally, it means, "I am who I am" or, "I will be what I will be." Most English-language Bibles translate it as "Lord".

Zeus: the Greek god of thunder, and the ruler of all the Greek gods.

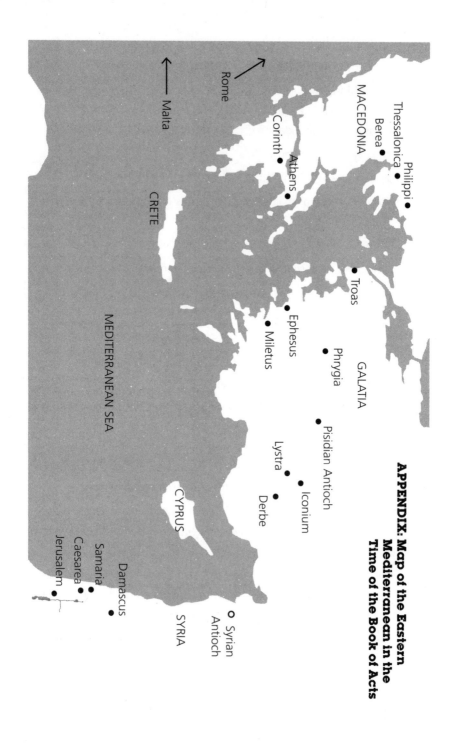

APPENDIX: Map of the Eastern
Mediterranean in the
Time of the Book of Acts

Rome

Malta

MACEDONIA
Thessalonica
Berea
Philippi

Corinth
Athens

CRETE

Troas

Ephesus
Miletus

Phrygia

GALATIA

Pisidian Antioch

Lystra
Iconium

Derbe

CYPRUS

MEDITERRANEAN SEA

Jerusalem
Caesarea
Samaria
Damascus

Syrian
Antioch

SYRIA

ACKNOWLEDGMENTS

I want to thank Lindy Robertson, Jr., a friend and fellow church member whose labor preserved my expository teaching through the book of Acts. His hard work of original transcription is much appreciated.

It has been a privilege to work with The Good Book Company on this project, and I appreciate Carl Laferton's work as editor. Here in Louisville, my writing projects are greatly assisted by the skill of my Director of Theological Research, Cory Higdon. A team of interns, including Mitchell Holley, David Lee, Ryan Loague, Bruno Sanchez, and Troy Solava, offered their own wisdom. All are greatly appreciated.

Acts 13–28 for...
Bible-study Groups

Albert Mohler's **Good Book Guide** to Acts 13–28 is the companion to this resource, helping groups of Christians to explore, discuss and apply Acts together. Eight studies, each including investigation, apply, getting personal, pray and explore more sections, take you through the second half of the book. Includes a concise Leader's Guide at the back.

Find out more at:
www.thegoodbook.com/goodbookguides

God's Word For You Series

- **Exodus For You** *Tim Chester*
- **Judges For You** *Timothy Keller*
- **1 Samuel For You** *Tim Chester*
- **2 Samuel For You** *Tim Chester*
- **Daniel For You** *David Helm*
- **Micah For You** *Stephen Um*
- **Luke 1-12 For You** *Mike McKinley*
- **Luke 12-24 For You** *Mike McKinley*
- **John 1-12 For You** *Josh Moody*
- **John 13-21 For You** *Josh Moody*
- **Acts 1-12 For You** *Albert Mohler*
- **Acts 13-21 For You** *Albert Mohler*
- **Romans 1-7 For You** *Timothy Keller*
- **Romans 8-16 For You** *Timothy Keller*
- **Galatians For You** *Timothy Keller*
- **Ephesians For You** *Richard Coekin*
- **Philippians For You** *Steven Lawson*
- **Colossians & Philemon For You** *Mark Meynell*
- **1 & 2 Timothy For You** *Phillip Jensen*
- **Titus For You** *Tim Chester*
- **James For You** *Sam Allberry*
- **1 Peter For You** *Juan Sanchez*
- **Revelation For You** *Tim Chester*

Find out more about these resources at:
www.thegoodbook.com/for-you

thegoodbook
COMPANY

BIBLICAL | RELEVANT | ACCESSIBLE

At The Good Book Company, we are dedicated to helping Christians and local churches grow. We believe that God's growth process always starts with hearing clearly what he has said to us through his timeless word—the Bible.

Ever since we opened our doors in 1991, we have been striving to produce Bible-based resources that bring glory to God. We have grown to become an international provider of user-friendly resources to the Christian community, with believers of all backgrounds and denominations using our books, Bible studies, devotionals, evangelistic resources, and DVD-based courses.

We want to equip ordinary Christians to live for Christ day by day, and churches to grow in their knowledge of God, their love for one another, and the effectiveness of their outreach.

Call us for a discussion of your needs or visit one of our local websites for more information on the resources and services we provide.

Your friends at The Good Book Company

thegoodbook.com | thegoodbook.co.uk
thegoodbook.com.au | thegoodbook.co.nz
thegoodbook.co.in